COACHING YOUTH BASKETBALL

KNACK

COACHING YOUTH BASKETBALL

Step-by-Step Strategy, Mechanics & Drills for Consistent Success

Kristen Somogyi

Photographs by Beth Balbierz

Guilford, Connecticut
An imprint of Globe Pequot Press

Copyright © 2010 by Morris Book Publishing, LLC

Editorial Director: Cynthia Hughes
Editor: Katie Benoit
Project Editor: Tracee Williams
Cover Design: Paul Beatrice, Bret Kerr
Interior Design: Paul Beatrice
Layout: Kevin Mak
Cover Photos by: Beth Balbierz
Interior Photos by: Beth Balbierz
Diagrams by Lorraine Enik
Diagram Vector Illustration © Gordan | Shutterstock

Library of Congress Cataloging-in-Publication Data
Somogyi, Kristen.
    Knack coaching youth basketball : step-by-step strategy, mechanics & drills for consistent success / Kristen Somogyi ; photographs by Beth Balbierz.
        p. cm.
    Includes index.
    ISBN 978-1-59921-952-3
    1. Basketball for children—Coaching. 2. Basketball—Coaching. I. Title.
    GV885.3.S67 2010
    796.323'62--dc22
                                        2010021235

The following manufacturers/names appearing in *Knack Coaching Youth Basketball* are trademarks:
Adidas®; AAU USA®; Coach™; Franklin®; Gatorade®; Johnson & Johnson®; KBA Big Ball™; NCAA®; Nike®; SPORTLINE®; Under Armour®; Wilson

Printed in China

10 9 8 7 6 5 4 3 2 1

Acknowledgments

This book wouldn't have been possible without the love and support from so many important people. Saying thank you is just a small part of how much you all mean to me. First I would like to thank my dad, John, mother, Nancy, sister, Jen, and my grandfather, Ed Burns. Thank you so much for years of special moments shared together. Thank you to the Central Jersey Cardinals Organization (parents and players) for your time and dedication for allowing us to shoot these pictures for several months. To the players I train, campers, and little Cardinals, thank you for letting me share in your growth as a player. To my coaches, thank you for your time and dedication. To Denise Girardi, Paul Byrnes, and Maureen Celoski for the countless hours spent on making the Cardinal program operate. Thank you to Rutgers Prep school, for allowing us to use your gym, without you there is no us. Thank you to Rahway Middle School for your patience and understanding when I was writing this book. Thank you to my two dear friends, Mary Klinger and Shannon Coyle for your support to me and always being there. At the end of the day when everyone has left the gym, you two are always there to lend a hand. That in itself says a lot about the type of friends you are. Thank you to my former high school coach, Ernie Vajda, and AAU Coach Karen "Fu" Fuccello, who has recently passed away. You are responsible for many of my personal basketball accomplishments. Special thanks to Beth Balbierz for all the Diet Cokes and of course the beautiful pictures capturing the essence the game. And to Patty Coyle for helping create the diagrams necessary for this book. If I have forgotten anyone blame my head, not my heart.

Photographer Acknowledgments

For my Mom: I Love You and Miss You!

I'd like to thank my family (Rob, Samantha, Derek, Dad and Amy) for all of your support and help in completing this project.

To Kristen: Thank you for writing this book and sharing your knowledge of the game of basketball with all of us. I know it was a challenge but well worth it in the end. So many more children will learn and appreciate the game thanks to you. I'm glad I had the chance to work with you after photographing you as a player. It's been great working with the best!

A huge thanks to the players, coaches and parents from the Central Jersey Cardinals, St. Matthias School, Franklin High School, and Rahway Middle School. I couldn't have done this without you.

I know I've tried your patience, especially toward the end, thank you Shannon!

Thank you to all the people at Rutgers Prep, Franklin High School, St. Mary's & St. Peter's Catholic Academy and Rahway Middle School, who let us use their facilities during the photographing of this book.

Finally, I'd like to thank Katie Benoit and Tracee Williams for all of their hard work in helping Kristen and me finish this book.

CONTENTS

INTRODUCTION

For me, coaching youth basketball has been one of the most enjoyable and worthwhile experiences of my life. Growing up in a basketball family, I learned at an early age that hard work and dedication can take you to immeasurable heights. From my own experience as a former player and as a coach, I am able to instill everything I learned in young athletes to help them be the best they can be.

One of the most exciting times of my career was breaking my own father's scoring record for the state of New Jersey. The story goes like this: My father, John Somogyi, set the New Jersey high school scoring record of 3,310 points during his high school career from 1964 to 1968. In 1992, while attending the same high school and wearing the same jersey number (twenty-four), I broke his record and ended my high school career with 3,899 points. The record still stands to this day. I never thought that I would one day break the scoring record set by the very person who day-in and day-out was my own personal coach and helped me be the best basketball player I could be.

It is safe to say that my high school experience and the coaches that taught me—Dad included—have had a profound impact on my life. I've coached players at all age levels, from six years old to high school level. My experience led me to start my own summer basketball camps, which currently host over 400 campers each summer. In addition, I founded one of the largest AAU programs in the state of New Jersey, called the Central Jersey Cardinals, which currently hosts twelve girls teams and two boys teams. Over the past several years, I've devoted my time to individually training athletes, from players trying to make a team to players going to college on full basketball scholarships.

Whatever the level, my passion, like all coaches' passions, is to make these athletes better players. I've coached undefeated teams, teams that never won a game, and teams that were beaten on a buzzer shot. Each year is a new and exciting challenge; every team, every practice, every camp, and every coaching experience is different each time. That's what makes coaching so special. Moments in sports come when least expected, like watching a player complete a simple layup with your encouragement or getting that winning basket. These are the times when coaches have the greatest influence on players. A pat on the back, a smile, or a high five may elevate a player's self-esteem and encourage him to go and achieve great things, and not just in the sport of basketball.

Coaching Today's Players

In today's game, the importance of perfecting skills tends to go by the wayside, often with too much emphasis put on game play. Players today are expected to play year-round, which can make them lose focus on developing their skills. In truth, players need to go back to basics and practice often and properly to become better players.

This is where *Knack Coaching Youth Basketball* steps in. This book provides players and coaches with necessary drills to improve their game. The book is broken down into three age groups for ease of coaching: six to nine years of age, ten to twelve years of age, and thirteen to fourteen years of age. It starts with basic skills, such as shooting, dribbling, and passing, and then moves into more advanced team drills. Chapters cover offensive and defensive sets, in-bound plays, press breakers, and last second shots. The book also covers practical matters, such as obtaining the proper equipment, learning the rules, and running tryouts. Many of these chapters will be helpful to a new coach just starting out.

The more advanced coach will find different strategies, plays, and tactics in this book to use in practice for older, more experienced players. The book will also address the advanced skills and strategies needed to become a

successful coach at more experienced playing levels. And, like with the brand new coach, even coaches who have been around the court a few times can do well with a refresher on how to work with and talk to parents, what to say during halftime talks, pregame reminders, and how to make the best use of gym time.

Continue Learning

My hope is that this book provides you with information that will make your coaching experience all the more rewarding,

Regardless of everything else, first and foremost, as coach, you have to work with the players that make up your team. Some teams develop on their own through great team chemistry and win championships, while others just don't quite get it and never pull together. However, the most important asset you have to these players is the ability to make sure they enjoy the sport and provide them with the necessary skills to become better players and people. And that's really what coaching youth sports is all about.

regardless of any hiccups along the road. Because, well, let's face it: You will make mistakes as a coach. Maybe you will call the wrong play; maybe you won't prepare your team enough; or maybe you won't play the right mix of players. There will be seasons where you will have plenty of talented players; seasons where your team struggles; and seasons where your team might be undersized. But remember, every coach can learn a little something from watching a practice, a game, or working a camp that will ultimately make him or her a better coach in the end and help the team be the best that it can be.

Keep It Positive

In the end, I'd like to leave you with two very important thoughts that I have learned over many years of coaching—one thought for the coach and one for the coach to convey to the players.

As a youth coach, your number one responsibility is to be one hundred percent concerned about the development of the individual player rather than the number of wins and losses. When it comes to development and ensuring that all players learn all parts of the game, there is a very delicate balance that you must maintain. Have all of your players learn and play all positions because you do not know the level of individual development and the potential size of the athlete.

When it comes to players, I have found that the most successful ones are those that are able to turn a negative situation into a positive one, not only in basketball, but also in the game of life. There no doubt will be many highs and lows in the game. However, players that are able to deal with adversity truly will succeed. If a player has a bad shooting night, then encourage her to find another way to contribute to the good of the team.

Above all else, when it comes to coaching, it is your responsibility to make the sport fun for young athletes. The ultimate reward in coaching is to ignite a spark in young players, who will then go on to develop a love for the game of basketball.

YOUR COACHING STYLE

Before you begin coaching, your practices, game routine, and schedule must be well organized

As coach you must develop your own coaching style. It's important that, whatever your style of coaching is, you be yourself. If you are outgoing, be outgoing; if you are laid-back and quiet, then continue to be that. Don't try to be something you're not. Instead, learn from successful coaches and incorporate their winning ways into your coaching philosophy.

Whatever your style is, remember you are also a teacher, a teacher not only of game skills but also, most importantly, of life skills. Be well prepared for practices and games. Encourage players, be in position, and have a passion for the game. If you come to practice enthusiastic, then players will be enthusiastic. Value every player on the team and treat all

Six- to Nine-year-old Players

- After you have decided to coach a team, determine which age level you will coach.

- Coaches must teach to the appropriate age level and understand the type of players they coach.

- Coaching players who are between six and nine years old requires patience and a lot of skill work.

- At this level the drills are basic, fun, and repetitive. Emphasis on rules should be taught at this time.

Ten- to Twelve-year-old Players

- At this age level players will have a year or two of basketball under their belts. They will begin to understand the game better and understand the different positions required.

- Players should know all necessary rules for the game.

- You can run basic plays that are comparable with their level of competition.

- You should emphasize proper sportsmanship. Teach players the value of winning and losing and help players develop a love for the game.

players equally. Make the last player on your team feel as important as your star player. This will build team chemistry. Don't forget about your assistant coaches and team managers. Everyone is important in the success of the team.

There are several general rules to obey when dealing with players, parents, assistants, and administrators: Be agreeable, easy to work with, but don't compromise your principles. Be respectful, follow the rules, and be easy to communicate with. Coaches must instill the concept of team rather than individual. Players must become unselfish in their thinking.

····· **GREEN ● LIGHT** ···········

Set rules and maintain discipline. Discipline is doing the right thing and doing everything to better the team. This means in practice doing every drill the right way every time. Players learn with repetition and consistency. Don't set too many rules; be flexible, consistent, and fair. Rules are rules; don't bend them for certain players.

Thirteen- to Fourteen-year-old Players

- At this level most players have tried out for their school team or participated in Amateur Athletic Union (AAU) competition.

- Players may have trained with a shooting coach and developed their own practice workouts.

- At this level players will be able to move to more advanced skills.

- You should help these players develop their physical and mental skills. Winning becomes important. Balance praise and criticism; too much of either can be harmful to a player.

Coaching Goals
- Players' skill development
- Team development
- Sportsmanship
- Fun
- Life skills/attitude

PARENT MEETING

Parents should give their child unconditional love, support, and encouragement

Communication with parents and guardians is key in making sure everyone's on the same page. Whether it's a meeting, handbook, phone call, or e-mail, expectations of the coach and team should be told to everyone involved.

A parent meeting should be set up before the season begins or on the first day of tryouts or practice. At the first meeting provide a handout to the parents. The handout should consist of your phone number, e-mail address and Web site (if available), goals and rules for the team, and a schedule of practices and games. A roster of players and phone numbers should be included along with the cost of the program, if there is any.

Parents' Role

- Remind parents that their children are participating to have fun, be with their friends, engage in friendly competition, and exercise.

- A parent's most important role is to provide his or her children with love, support, and encouragement. Give them the freedom to play and enjoy the game.

- Most parents criticize their children as soon as the children make a mistake. Instead, parents should let their children have fun and enjoy the game at their own pace. Pressure will only hinder their progress.

Web Site/E-mail

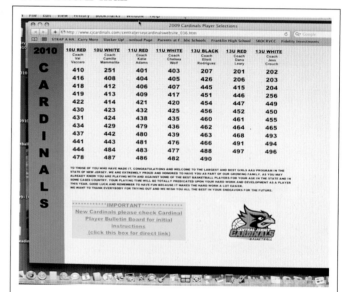

- E-mail is an important tool for getting out timely information, such as game schedules or directions.

- A Web site is useful as a central location to post events and accomplishments. Players enjoy seeing their picture up on the Web and visiting the site.

- The type of organization or league that you coach in will help determine the need for a Web site.

- Text messages—a child's equivalent of phone calls—are also a useful tool for getting information out quickly.

After all the necessary paperwork is complete, go over your policy about playing time with the parents. Remember that winning is not the primary concern at the youth age level. The league that your team plays in will determine the playing time. Almost all Catholic Youth Organization (CYO)/travel leagues have a standard substitution pattern. Explain excused and unexcused absences so that parents are clear. It's unfair for a player to consistently miss practice and be guaranteed playing time. Some type of guidelines must be established for the team.

When dealing with parents be honest and open and show them you really care about their child. Be available before and after games to answer any questions and concerns. Parents want the best for their kids, so it's best not to ignore the parents. If you have a son or daughter on the team, be fair. Treat your child as if he or she were any other player on the team. Don't overplay or overcriticize your child. Establish the coach/player rapport during the time spent on the basketball court and leave it on the court.

Sportsmanship

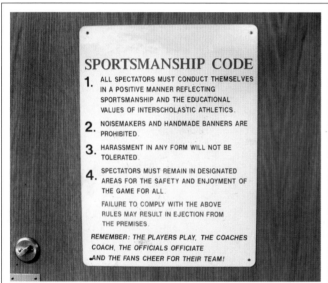

- Teach sportsmanship to your players through your example: No yelling at the refs, no demeaning the other team, other players, and so forth.

- Teach players to respect their opponents and to play hard, not dirty, and to respect the officials.

- Parents will have varying perspectives while watching games. Some parents will give "win only" advice from the sidelines, whereas others simply will be thankful that their child is on the team.

- Whatever the case, parents should conduct themselves with good sportsmanship.

Coach/Parent/Player Relationships

- Make yourself available at all times for interaction between the parents and the players.

- Parents should be able to come to you for advice and guidance.

- Whether to allow parents at practice will be a decision made by you. Determine at the beginning of the season if practices are open or closed.

- Remind parents that if they are at practice they must keep quiet and not "coach" their kids from the stands.

TEAM MEETING
Planning is an essential part of coaching success

After your team is established a meeting is necessary. Your official team meeting will come after members of your team have been picked or registration has taken place. This meeting can be before practice starts or on a separate day. During the team meeting, rules and expectations will be given. You should give a brief personal background of your coaching and playing experience. I encourage this because it's personal and because kids enjoy hearing about their coach. Each player should also introduce himself or herself and give a brief description of what he or she is like. Don't embarrass players if they are shy. Maybe ask them questions to get them to talk.

After rules are set and particulars about the schedule and practice times are understood, then you can talk about your expectations with your staff. This meeting should not involve any parents, only assistant coaches and team managers. All questions should be answered at this time.

Coaching Players

- Let kids know that it is okay to make mistakes and that you expect them to make mistakes along the way. All players and coaches make mistakes; players just need to learn to keep playing hard and to learn from these mistakes.

- Do not embarrass players because doing so creates more stress and can turn a player away from the sport.

- If a specific player makes a mistake, address it as a group and do not pinpoint the player. Alternately, take the player aside and address the problem then.

Important Papers

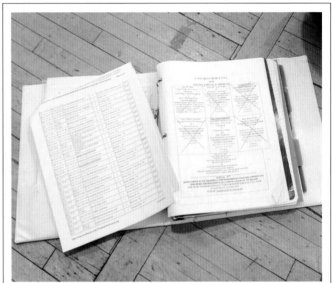

- There are important papers to keep with you. These include medical release forms, registration forms, practice schedules, game schedules, and important phone numbers.

- A folder with these papers in it should be carried at all times.

- I suggest supplying the team manager with the same papers.

- Your practice plan should also be with you at all times, as well as the practice plan from the week before so you can refer back to it.

As the season progresses, team gatherings should start and end practice. Practice should begin with a few goals that you want to accomplish in practice along with general reminders. Compliments and constructive criticism about plays during the previous game or practice can be given to the players at this time.

At the end of practice bring players together to review what was done during the session and to reiterate a few general reminders. Always end in a huddle with hands together to cheer out loud.

You can call a team meeting at anytime during the season. Sometimes a team meeting is needed to bring the team members back together and regroup. This can be necessary if a team is winning or losing. Show your team members that you care by explaining to them what is needed to win the remaining games or to beat a particular team you haven't previously beaten.

Contact Information

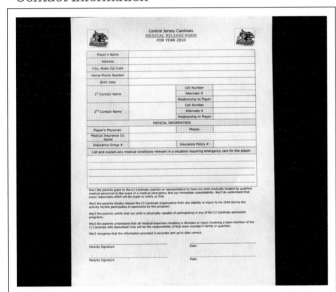

- Each player must fill out forms with his or her contact information.

- This information should be the player's name, address, e-mail address, cell phone number, home number, grade, and age.

- Other important information should be provided as well, such as the name of an emergency contact, medical issues, and allergies.

- Information that is less important but necessary to some organizations include the player's T-shirt size, sneaker size, uniform number, and payment plan.

Team Players

- Encourage players to respect and cheer for each other.

- Some players are natural leaders, and players will tend to follow them. These players are typically first in line and are outgoing. They lead by example.

- As players get older, captains can be chosen by teammates. Coaches should not pick captains unless a captain causes problems and doesn't deserve to be in that position.

EXPECTATIONS OF COACH
Proper planning of preseason and in-season activities is necessary

You are the leader and the mentor of your team and as a result carry many responsibilities. After your players lace up their sneakers, every member of your team has a job to do. Everyone owes it to each other to practice and compete as hard as he or she can. As a coach, you must prepare your team to foster a great work ethic. After establishing a great work ethic, you must then provide your team members with the necessary skill set to become the very best they can. Prepare

a practice plan everyday by selecting drills that are tailored to your game style and deal with strengths and weaknesses of players. By making practices competitive and hard every day, you should have no surprises when the actual games are played. As the season progresses, your practices might change so you can prepare for an upcoming game based on your observations of another team.

Your players' style of play will be determined a lot by what

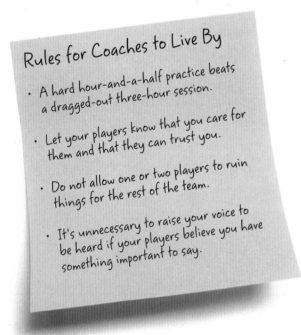

Rules for Coaches to Live By

- A hard hour-and-a-half practice beats a dragged-out three-hour session.

- Let your players know that you care for them and that they can trust you.

- Do not allow one or two players to ruin things for the rest of the team.

- It's unnecessary to raise your voice to be heard if your players believe you have something important to say.

Motivating Players

- As coach, you must be prepared and willing to put in the effort. Coaches lead by example. If a coach doesn't care, neither will players.

- In practice, players will stay motivated if drills are competitive and not boring. Too much standing around will allow players to talk to teammates, sit down, and not pay attention. Keep everyone engaged at all times.

- Move quickly from one drill to the next; do not spend half of your practice time on one drill.

type of players you have. For example, if you have quick, athletic players who like to run, then an up-tempo style of play might be ideal for your team. This style involves executing fast breaks, pressing, and trapping. If your team has a strong inside game and likes the half-court-style game, then a slow pace is ideal. Some years you will have great players; some years you won't. Be flexible and cater to the needs of your team. Many of the same drills and plays will be used from year to year. Be sure to stress the importance of putting in a winning effort all the time.

You must instill the concept of team in your players. Team chemistry will develop throughout the season. You must make the players believe in each other and in a common team goal.

Teaching

- Teaching is critical at the youth level. Teach basic fundamentals, such as dribbling, making layups, and shooting.

- Take your time in practice and thoroughly explain each drill. Demonstrate drills as well as explain why the drills are important.

- Remember that teaching is a progression. Kids will get better. Drills must be repetitive and taught correctly each time.

- You constantly must correct mistakes. Don't assume that players know how to do drills correctly.

Team Unity

- Team unity develops throughout the season. It comes from small celebrations and odd moments when least expected.

- Sometimes it's a last-second shot being made or a player falling down in practice that results in team unity. A good laugh during practice is sometimes needed.

- Always end practice with an upbeat moment, whether it's shooting at half court or challenging an assistant coach or manager to make a shot. This allows the team members to encourage each other and then to celebrate accomplishments.

EXPECTATIONS OF PLAYERS
Be sure players are committed to the team and willing to improve

Your expectations of players will vary during the season, but one thing that will never vary is your expectation of them to work hard and to play to the best of their abilities. Players are expected to attend all practices and games on time and to be prepared with the proper gear, sneakers, and uniform. They should be prepared to be in good condition and ready to learn and listen. Players with good attitudes who play tough defense will gain the respect of coaches and teammates. No one likes hot dogs or players who turn the ball over or exude bad attitudes.

During games players are expected to have knowledge of the rules of the game. They should show up thirty minutes prior to game time wearing the proper game-day uniform and sneakers. Players are expected to cheer for teammates when the teammates are on the floor.

A player's preparation pertains to off the court as well.

Cheering

- Teams develop high fives, handshakes, and chants during games and practice.

- High fives always occur during games. They are a nice way to say "Great job" to a teammate.

- Players often clap together during warm-ups.

- Players on the bench motivate their teammates by chanting popular phrases, such as "Defense!"

- This type of cheering goes a long way to motivate, especially when fans get involved.

Staying Focused

- When planning, you should divide the season into three parts: Preseason, in-season, and postseason.

- Preseason drills will be different than drills in the in-season and postseason. Players need a focused mind-set for each part of the season.

- When you break the season into manageable parts, players stay focused and accomplish small goals.

Players should be required to get good grades in class in order to play and should be role models outside of the game. And players need to have a strong work ethic by working extra both during the regular season and the off-season. Players should eat properly. Nutritious foods and adequate hydration are a must for athletes. Encourage parents to provide water and sports drinks for their children. Remind players to rest and drink a lot of fluids.

On the court players are expected to tell a you when they are hurt or sick. They should ask for extra help if they don't understand a play or drill. As coach, don't assume they understand. Players need direction and repetition. Take time to show players the correct way to do things even if you repeat yourself. It's rewarding when a player finally gets the game.

Working Hard

- Players are expected to work hard every time they step onto the floor.

- As a coach, you must bring this hard work ethic out in all players and help them become the best players they can be.

- Practice must be harder than the games. Games should then be fun.

- Hard work will result in games being won and players getting better.

- Hard work from all parties—coaches, players, and managers—is required for the success of the team.

Coming Prepared

- Preparation is the key to success.

- Players need to physically and mentally prepare themselves for practice and game play.

- Players need to be in good physical condition, eat properly, and get rest.

- They must have the proper practice and game attire. Girl basketball players should pull up their hair into a ponytail and make sure all jewelry is off before games start.

- Proper sneakers with good ankle protection are also necessary.

GETTING TO KNOW YOUR TEAM

Learn your team's strengths and weaknesses through a series of activities

Your relationship with your players will be a rewarding experience. Giving players respect and working hard for them will result in a positive atmosphere throughout the season. Being a successful coach requires hard work and dedication. If your players see you doing just that, they will follow and respond to your lead. You are with these players for several months; getting to know them in a short period of time is critical in developing team chemistry.

Some coaches will practice every day. Typically middle school teams have practice for two hours every day from November to February. This gives coaches an excellent opportunity to develop team chemistry and to developing players' skills. This

Younger Players

- Younger players who first start out need guidance.

- They have a short attention span, so drills need to be easy and fun.

- These players will run around a lot, become excited when a basket is made, and are very big on keeping score.

- They need specific direction. You need to be on the court during practice and to walk them through drills. Assistant coaches are needed at this level.

Middle-aged Players

- Rules and knowledge of the game will start to develop around ten to twelve years of age. Players will start to mature and to learn specific positions.

- Practice, along with drills, still needs to be fun, but game play can be incorporated at this time.

- At this level you will see certain players with better skills. These players tend to have the ball often and score the majority of the points. As a coach, make sure all players get involved.

is an ideal situation. However, many travel, CYO, and recreation teams do not have this opportunity. These teams are lucky to get in two practices a week. Practices typically last for an hour and a half. Many times gyms are shared, and there just isn't enough time to get everything accomplished.

As coach, you need to maximize all your practice time and have specific time for drills and game situations incorporated into your practice plan. You must learn every player's name and his or her strengths and weaknesses. Get to know players off the court as well. Make yourself available to be at practice early or to stay after to provide extra help. You can learn a lot about a player in just fifteen extra minutes.

Schedule fun games once in a while to develop team chemistry and have light practices here and there so your players can enjoy each other. Know players' personalities. Some players are more sensitive than others; some players can take constructive criticism; and some players need confidence and positive reinforcement. If you are fair, honest, and constant, then you never have to second guess the decisions you make that are best for the team.

Older Players

- This age group will start to develop team strategies and improve their skills with more advanced drills.

- Winning becomes important because players develop a sense of team and expect teammates to fulfill their roles.

- Players begin to train outside of their regular practices on conditioning and strength training.

Various Sizes of Players

- Players come in different heights and weights. Some tall, some small, some are muscular, and some not.

- All players, no matter what size, should be taught the fundamentals of the game.

- As players get older and grow, specific positions will be tailored to their body structure. Small players tend to be guards, whereas taller players play inside.

- Players at a young age should take turns trying different positions. As a coach, you never know if a child will get taller or stay the same height.

BASIC GEAR

There are two types of basketballs—men's and women's balls and indoor and outdoor balls

In basketball certain equipment is necessary to play the sport. The most important equipment is, of course, the basketball. The basketball is a round orange or brown ball made of rubber or leather. Basketballs come in various sizes for different levels of play.

Many outdoor basketballs have different colors and designs.

In an official game, however, the ball must meet regulations. The shape of the ball must be round, and the color must be orange or light brown. The ball will have either eight or twelve seams. Originally a soccer ball was used to play the game. The ball then was changed and colored orange to make it visible to the players.

Junior Ball

- The junior ball is 27.5 inches in circumference and comes in a variety of colors and patters. This ball is also called a "size 5."

- It should be used only for players ages six to nine.

- Young players' hands are small, so dribbling, shooting, and passing are harder with the regular-size ball. Allow young players to have success with the junior ball until they feel comfortable using the women's ball.

- Have both junior and women's balls at practice. Note that junior balls will not be used in games.

Women's Ball

- The women's basketball was introduced to the game in 1988. Before that time a men's ball was used. The ball was changed to make it easier for women to shoot and dribble.

- The ball is 28.5 inches in circumference and weighs 20 ounces. It is recommended for kids ten years old and older. The women's ball is the official game ball for women's high school, college, and the Women's National Basketball Association (WNBA). The ball is also called a "size 6."

A regular, or men's, basketball is 29.5 inches in circumference; a women's ball is 28.5 inches; and a junior ball is 27.5 inches. Many youth leagues play with the women's ball until seventh grade. Then these leagues use the men's ball. Women continue to play with the women's ball no matter what the age. The women's ball has the number 28.5 printed on it. Junior balls are used for beginner players with small hands because these players have a hard time shooting the larger ball.

ZOOM

Encourage younger players to use the junior ball when they are starting out. Simply making a basket will develop their confidence. A junior ball is easier to control when dribbling. Players will eventually pick up a regular-size ball on their own and begin to use it.

Men's Ball

- Basketballs come in a variety of sizes, depending on level of play.

- The men's basketball is 29.5 inches in circumference and weighs 22 ounces. This is the official game ball for men's high school, college, and professional play. The ball is called a "size 7."

- The men's ball is recommended for high school play on, however many leagues start using the men's ball in seventh grade.

Ball Bag, Rack, Pump

- A ball bag is necessary for transporting basketballs to and from gyms. Many times the gym belongs to another school or is rented out. Keep track of all basketballs—they can get away easily!

- Middle school teams usually have ball racks. These racks are wheeled out so players can take balls from them. They are an easy way to store basketballs. Make sure the rack is always locked up at the end of practice.

- An air pump is necessary to have in case a ball goes flat.

SMALL GEAR

Check the condition of equipment, training devices, and court before practice and games begin

Coaches are responsible for bringing necessary equipment to practices and games. Besides bringing basketballs, you need to bring other small gear. The most obvious item a coach needs is a whistle. Whistles are used in practice, but never in games. Blowing a whistle tells players when to stop a certain drill and gains their attention. Youth players need direction and signals. Having a whistle will make your job much easier and save your voice.

Cones are a useful training tool to use in practice. Cones provide boundaries that tell players where to go. Cones can be used in several dribbling drills. Younger players can dribble around—and weave through—cones for ball control practice.

Whistle

- You should purchase a whistle before the season begins. Whistles are cheap and come in a variety of school or team colors.

- Purchase a lanyard to hold the whistle around your neck so the whistle isn't lost.

- Blow the whistle in a forceful manner to get the attention of players. Avoid blowing the whistle at every instance. Whistles should be blown when necessary, not for every drill.

- Whistles also help you referee when your players scrimmage against each other in practice.

Cones

- Cones are necessary equipment for practices. They come in different sizes and colors. Purchasing a set of ten is ideal.

- Cones are great for teaching younger players to dribble. Players must dribble around cones and keep their head up.

- Cones provide boundaries that help show younger players where to go on the court.

- Cones can be used for shooting drills. Have players do cuts around them or at them.

Clipboards are mostly used in games during timeouts or at halftime. All clipboards have the outline of the basketball court. Some are dry-erase, whereas others are magnetic. You should always have a clipboard ready during timeouts.

Other necessary items are pinnies. Pinnies are loose tank tops. They should be of the same color. Players wear pinnies to indicate they are on the same team. Pinnies can be shared when substitution occurs and help younger players identify who is on their team.

Some teams are fortunate to have practice jerseys. Practice jerseys are reversible and can be worn over T-shirts. Each player has a jersey so he or she doesn't have to share. I recommend investing in practice jerseys for older players. Older players will sweat more and will not want to share. Coaches should wash pinnies as much as possible. Buying a set of ten, at least, is ideal.

Clipboard

- A clipboard is great for diagramming and demonstrating a play during a timeout, before a game, or at halftime.

- The clipboard can be dry-erase or magnetic. Magnetic clipboards allow you to move around small magnet circles to simulate players.

- I recommend dry-erase because the back of the board can be used to write important reminders for the game.

Pinnies and Practice Jerseys

- Pinnies come in a variety of colors and are made of mesh material.

- Pinnies are loose tank tops used to help players distinguish their teammates.

- These shirts are shared among teammates and therefore must be washed after each practice.

- Practice jerseys are reversible shirts and used like pinnies, but each player has his or her own.

- Each player is responsible for his or her practice jersey. Jerseys can be worn over T-shirts, too.

MORE SMALL GEAR
A few little aids can make a big difference

A stopwatch, water bottles, a water cooler, and a scoreboard are additional items that are helpful at practices and games. Stopwatches come in handy when timing a drill. Typically a team drill will last three to five minutes. Individual drills are timed in sequences ranging from thirty seconds to two minutes. Employing a stopwatch allows players to get equal time and keep drills moving.

Throughout practice water breaks are needed. Most of the time players bring their own water or sports drinks. A water cooler can be provided for players during practice and games. However, many teams use other schools to practice in, and coaches don't have access to water coolers. In these cases instead use reusable water bottles, which are easy to carry and fill.

If you don't have the ability to bring refreshments, remind players to bring their own water bottle or sports drink. At the

Stopwatch

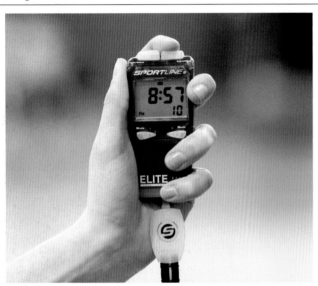

- A stopwatch can be a dedicated timepiece or a function of a wristwatch.

- Stopwatches are necessary to have in practice. Create competition by timing different drills to make practice both fun and challenging.

- Each practice should be planned down to the last minute. Drills should be done in a timely manner.

- If a scoreboard is available, make use of it. Players like to see how much time is left when being timed.

Water Bottles

- Reusable water bottles are easy to carry and fill.

- Some water bottles have their own carrying cases that holds six bottles to make it easier to carry to games.

- If preferred, players may bring their own water or sports drink.

- Players should not share water bottles. Rather, encourage them to bring their own drinks or ask parents to bring drinks to games.

very least, all gyms will have water fountains; however, many leagues provide refreshments for players who don't bring their own.

A flip scoreboard or tabletop electronic scoreboard can be useful for scrimmages. Many times you won't have access to wall-mounted scoreboards. If your team invites another team to scrimmage, a scoreboard should be provided.

EQUIPMENT

Water Coolers

- Water coolers can be made available to players for refreshments instead of players bringing their own. Cups are provided, or players can fill their own water bottles.

- Many gyms do not provide water coolers. As players get older and enter high school, more teams provide coolers in their gyms.

- Water coolers are cumbersome to carry to away games. Regardless, some type of water station must be provided during practices and games.

Scoreboards

- Wall scoreboards are operated manually by a keyboard at a table. These scoreboards usually operate during games.

- Electronic tabletop scoreboards are often used when several games are being played in one gym. These scoreboards are operated right at the table and show points, time, and fouls.

- A flip scoreboard can be used in practice. This scoreboard does not record time but is good for keeping track of the score. A person manually flips a numbered card over when a basket is scored.

COACHING ATTIRE
Be professional and dress the part, whether for a practice or for a game

You should wear different attire for practices and games. Leagues don't typically have dress codes, so what you wear is up to you. However, a level of professionalism comes with coaching. Your coaching location and level determine what you should wear. Some leagues hold games outdoors; some gyms are cooler than others. Some are air conditioned.

A comfortable, loose-fitting outfit is ideal for practices. A T-shirt and sweat pants or track pants are perfectly suitable. Coaches should wear sneakers, and clothes should be loose to move around. Practices typically last for an hour and a half, and you will be on your feet, so you want to be comfortable. Basketball is played during the winter months; a sweatshirt

Male Coach Game Attire

- On game day male coaches should wear a nice pair of pants with a collared sports shirt or a sweater.

- A nice comfortable pair of shoes should go with the outfit.

- Other attire options include a matching jogging suit with a clean pair of sneakers.

- During the warmer months a branded T-shirt with a pair of khaki shorts is ideal.

- Shirts should be tucked in, and hats should not be worn.

Female Coach Game Attire

- Female coaches should wear a comfortable jogging suit or a collared shirt with a pair of sports pants and a clean pair of sneakers during a game.

- Avoid wearing anything tight or high heels. Although such attire looks nice, you will be uncomfortable throughout the game.

- If your team advances to championship play, or there's a big game between two teams, wearing a nice pair of pants and a sweater is ideal.

- If your athletic department provides you with pullover jackets or shirts, those items are also acceptable.

or long-sleeve shirt will keep you warm. Coaches who coach AAU and summer camps should dress according to weather.

Game attire is similar to practice attire; however, a nice collared shirt is recommended. Coaches need to be comfortable. A matching jogging suit with a jacket is also suitable. Clean sneakers should be worn. Some coaches wear a shirt and tie if their team advances to championship play, and many encourage "dressing up" among their staff and players for game days.

Male Coach Practice Attire

- There really is no rule for dress attire for practice other than wearing dress that is neat and practical.

- Comfort is a must during practice. You will be demonstrating drills and showing players what to do throughout practice, so you need to be comfortable.

- I suggest wearing a T-shirt under a sweatshirt or long-sleeve shirt in case you get hot.

- Always wear comfortable sneakers.

Female Coach Practice Attire

- There is no female dress code when it comes to practice.

- Gyms tend to be hot even during the winter months. Wearing shorts or a T-shirt under a jogging suit allows you to take off the pants or jacket if you work up a sweat.

- There will be times in practice when you might have to partner up with a player or show a drill that requires moving.

- Female coaches should pull their hair back so it doesn't get in the way during practice.

IMPORTANT COACH'S EQUIPMENT
Be organized and be prepared

Besides the necessary equipment for games and practices, you must carry your own important items. A coaching bag should be separate from the bag used to carry the basketballs. A coaching bag should contain important player information, a small first-aid kit, a scorebook, cones, and a clipboard. You should not bring all these items to games. Rather, use separate bags for games and for practices.

A practice plan is necessary to keep track of your team's development and skills taught in each practice. A practice plan allows your team to be organized and to accomplish the day's agenda. A daily plan should be typed up and given to your coaching staff, so that all staff members are on the same page. If you plan on coaching long term, keep practice plans over the years so you can look back at your notes and see which drills were done at different times of the season.

Player information should be kept in a folder and taken with

Coaching Bag

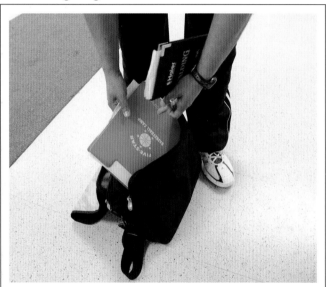

- Never leave home without your coaching bag.

- The bag should contain all equipment needed for games and practices, including your scorebook, player information, and personal equipment.

- After the game is over do not allow players to see your scorebook. When players compare points, a selfish atmosphere can result.

Practice Plans

- Practice plans should have a list of goals that needs to be accomplished daily during practice.

- The plans should include time to do drills, time to run plays, and time to scrimmage at the end.

- During practice take notes and reminders for next practice to help in accomplishing your team's goals.

- Keep practice plans after the season is over. Save them on your computer or in a file so you can refer to them when needed.

you at all times. This information should have contact numbers and medical history in case of an emergency. A team mom should also have a copy of this information.

Taping games and practices is a useful practice that allows players to see their strengths and weaknesses. If a parent volunteers to videotape games, this is a bonus. Kids love seeing themselves, and coaches can point out events that happened throughout the game. A nice gift for players at the end of the year is a video of the best moments of the season. It's a great keepsake that players and family members can enjoy.

•••••••••••••••• GREEN ● LIGHT ••••••••••••••••

Update all equipment, scorebooks, and the current roster during the season. Be sure to update any changes of address or telephone numbers of players. After the end of season, look into purchasing new equipment for the following year. It's always nice to have new equipment to start a new season.

Folders

- Being organized as a coach makes your life much easier. Although collecting paperwork in the beginning of the season can be a hassle, this information will be useful in the case of an emergency.

- Make sure parents fill out all information for their children, including medical history. Many school teams require a full physical before players can play, and leagues may also require parent permission and medical clearance.

- Make copies of paperwork for assistants and team parents in case you are unable to make an emergency call.

Videotape

- Videotaping games or practices is a useful practice; it allows you to observe how other teams play and to watch your own team.

- Videotaping games or practices should be done sporadically. Doing so will benefit your team.

- After a game watch the video with your players so you can explain plays. Pause the video to let players see their mistakes. Be positive when showing a game video, but be sure to point out different mistakes. Avoid criticizing the same players.

OTHER TRAINING DEVICES

Help players strengthen and condition their bodies

Training devices have become popular in recent years. Some work, whereas others do not. Using different training devices can help players in many areas of the game, and there are generally two types of devices: Devices that help with body conditioning and devices that help with skill sets. Training devices that are used to help with conditioning and strengthening the body differ from basketball skill training devices. All devices, however, can be used at any time during the season, not just in the off-season.

"Blinders," as one example, are a training device for younger players learning to dribble. Blinders are glasses that prevent players from looking down at the basketball. There are also training devices that improve other skill sets, such as shooting. Some devices help keep a player from turning his wrist and teach the player to not drop his hand when shooting. These devices are okay to teach proper hand placement, but

Big Basketball

- The "big basketball" is not to be confused with the "weighted basketball."

- The big basketball comes in both men's and women's sizes. The weight of the ball is the same as that of a regulation ball, but the ball is bigger, making it harder to handle.

- This ball is great for ball-handling and shooting drills. The larger size helps players palm the ball better. All drills can be done with this ball. Players should not change shots or dribble when using this ball.

Blinders for Dribbling

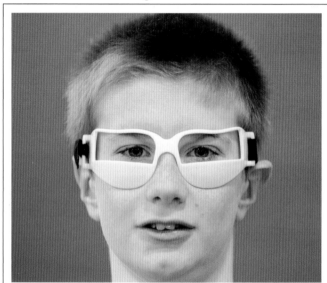

- Blinders are thick goggles that cover the eyes or have plastic rims that extend below the eyes.

- Blinders prevent players from looking down at the ball as they dribble.

- Although players may look silly, blinders are a great training device to help younger kids break the habit.

- These goggles are inexpensive and can be shared among your players.

remember that these devices cannot be used in the game, so the player must be weaned off the devices.

Some devices are simple. Place a portable soccer goal or something tall in front of a player to demonstrate how to shoot over an object. Younger players tend to jump forward when they shoot. Place an object in front of a player to have her jump the correct way.

Of course, the training devices and equipment you use depend on the individual player, level, and team.

The shooting gun, as an example of a more advanced device, is used to pass out basketballs to players. It is an expensive device that has to stay in the gym and may not be available to all coaches. Shooting guns give players many shots without the players having to rebound; they simulate game passes. Basketballs are set to a timer, so different cuts can be performed before the balls come out.

Then there are body-conditioning devices. Agility ladders, weighted balls, and jump ropes are other training devices that help older players improve their strength and conditioning.

Ladders/Weighted Balls

- Ladders and weighted balls are good strength and conditioning tools for players to use during preseason and off-season.

- Ladders laid flat on the floor develop foot speed along with coordination and conditioning. Ladders help players move fast and stay on the balls of their feet by jumping in and out of the rungs.

- Weighted balls can be used for doing passing drills and working on core strength. Weighted balls are hard to catch and throw. Players pass the weighed ball to each other to develop arm strength.

Rebounding Pads

- Rebounding pads are soft pads with holders on the back for coaches to put their hands into.

- Rebounding pads are used to block the player as he goes up for a shot or gets a rebound.

- The coach stands under the basket, and the pad makes contact with the player's body. This contact forces the player to go up strong to the basket. Players can be blocked multiple times in a controlled manner.

OBJECT OF THE GAME
Learn the sport before you start coaching

The game of basketball was invented by Dr. James Naismith in 1891. The object of the game is to outscore your opponent by putting the ball through the opponent's basket.

Dr. Naismith, Physical Education Director, invented basketball as an indoor sport to help keep students active during the winter months. Today basketball is played predominantly inside. However, many outdoor summer leagues, camps, clinics, and pickup games are played on outdoor courts.

The game was originally played with a peach basket at each end of the court. After a player shot a basket, a person stood on a ladder and took the ball out of the basket. Since then many rules of the game have changed to speed up the game. Basketball has become one of the most popular sports in the country. Why? There are several reasons: Basketball can be played alone, with a few friends, or on a team. It's one of the easiest sports to find a place to play; basketball equipment is

The Basket and Backboard

- The basket, or rim, is placed in the middle of the backboard. A square box is painted on the backboard to help players aim for the box and, subsequently, the basket.

- Have young players aim for the painted box when they shoot.

- The rim extends out from the backboard and is exactly 10 feet from the ground.

- A white net hangs from the rim to slow the ball as it goes through the hoop, giving the opposing team time to take the ball out of bounds.

The Basketball Hoop

- A basketball hoop can be shaped like a rectangle or a fan.

- The backboard is typically made of fiberglass or wood.

- The basketball hoop is either mounted on a wall and extended out to the court or mounted on top of

- a 10-foot padded pole.

- Portable basketball hoops can be wheeled out onto court. Their baskets can be lowered for beginner use.

- Outside basketball hoops have double rims and chain nets for weather purposes.

minimal; and there are nearly unlimited numbers of leagues, from recreation CYO and travel to school team and AAU.

Basketball is played worldwide by both sexes and people of all ages. A team is made up of ten to twelve players. Only five players from each team are allowed on the court at a time. Ideally there is a head coach and an assistant coach on the bench. A team is organized, guided, and instructed by the coach.

The easiest way to teach young players the rules of the sport is to explain what is not allowed versus what is allowed. The best way to teach the object of the game is to demonstrate the different parts of the game and make corrections and offer advice as the players practice.

The Court Breakdown

- Knowing basketball jargon and spacing on the court allows players to position themselves in certain areas.

- Point: Top of the key area, almost back to the jump ball circle.

- Wing: Two areas on both sides of the key, just inside the three-point line.

- Block: The square box outside the lane area.

- High post: Foul line area extending to the elbow.

- Paint: The area inside the key, which is a solid color of paint.

The Scoreboard

- A good scoreboard shows points, time, fouls, and possessions.

- The scoreboard varies from gym to gym.

- Scoreboards can be mounted to a wall and controlled electronically by the scorekeeper at the table.

- A tabletop electronic scoreboard also can be operated by the scorekeeper.

- A possession arrow will be at the scorekeeper's table. When a jump ball occurs, the referee refers to the possession arrow.

RULES

Understand and reinforce general rules so that your players properly learn the game

As a coach, you need to learn many of the basic rules of the game. Your league's rules might be modified for its level of play. These rules, such as substitution, length of game, and foul shots, vary with different age groups. Younger players use basketballs of a different size, and portable basketball hoops that can be lowered are also available in some gyms.

Players learn best when rules are strictly enforced and repeated. Don't let simple rules such as those regarding traveling and double dribbling fall by the wayside. Make the correction every time in practice so that when game time comes, the player can focus on other parts of the game.

Basketball originally had only thirteen rules. However, many

Possessions

- When a player breaks one of the rules of basketball, a violation occurs, and the ball goes to the opposing team. Here are some common violations:

- Traveling: Occurs when a player takes more than two steps without bouncing the ball.

- Double dribble: Occurs when a player stops dribbling and then starts dribbling again.

- Jump ball: Occurs when two players are tied up grabbing for the ball and possession is unclear. The possession arrow will determine who gets the ball.

Substitution

- Substitution occurs when a player replaces another player on the court.

- All entering players must report to the score table and squat down, ready to go into the game after play is stopped.

- A player might be subbed out because he is not producing, the player has been hurt or become tired, or the player does not understand what to do.

- Many leagues require that at the four-minute mark all players must come out of the game and a new set of five players must go in.

rules have been added. The rules are generally consistent across all levels and leagues, whether you play in pickup games or in organized games. Every game starts with a jump ball at the center of the court. A referee tosses the ball up into the air while one player from each team tries to tap the ball to teammates circled around mid-court.

The length of the game varies depending on the level. Recreational, grade, and high school games last thirty-two minutes (four quarters of eight minutes each). The clock stops for every dead ball based on the referee's call. Possession of the ball alternates from offense to defense.

Good defense will force the other team's offense to miss a shot or lose possession. Good offense will move the ball around while running through plays to try to score. The ball is advanced by dribbling or passing it up the court. If a game is tied at the end of regulation time, the two teams play an overtime period of three minutes. Play continues until a team finishes the period with more points than the other team.

Fouls

- Fouls are committed by both offensive and defensive players but mostly defensive players.

- Play stops when fouls are committed.

- Common fouls include blocking, reaching in, fouling while shooting, charging, holding, illegal screening, and over-the-back.

- A foul has one of two consequences: The fouled player will shoot foul shots, or the opposing team will get possession of the ball. These fouls typically occur when the player is not in the act of shooting.

Timeouts

- Coaches and players can call timeouts several times per half.

- Timeouts are called to set up plays or to give the players a rest and a water break.

- Timeouts called by the referee aren't deducted from the number allotted to teams. A referee may call a timeout when a player is hurt, an object is on the court, a fan commits unsportsmanlike conduct, or the scorekeeper has an issue.

- Timeouts can be called only by the team that has possession of the ball.

BASKETBALL DIMENSIONS
Know the long and the short of the court

Basketball court dimensions vary slightly according to levels. However, all basketball courts have many similar features. The court itself is 94 feet long and 50 feet wide. The average playing area for recreational and grade school is 84 feet long by 50 feet wide. The hoop is 10 feet above the ground. The point line is 19 feet 9 inches from the basket. The foul line is 15 feet from the basket.

The backboard aids players in shooting the basketball into the hoop and prevents the ball from going out of bounds. The rim itself is 18 inches in diameter. Each basket has a white, nylon-mesh net that hangs down about 15 inches from the rim.

The height of the basket can be adjusted according to grade level. For six- to nine-year-olds, the height of 8 feet is ideal. Ten- to thirteen-year-olds should be able to reach the standard 10-foot basket.

Full Court

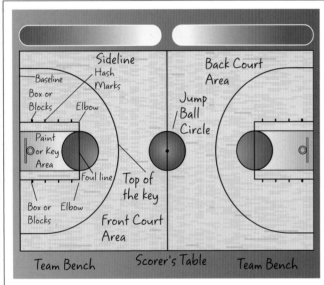

Half Court

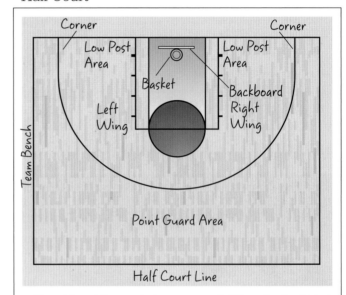

- The basketball court is made up of several areas. Knowing these areas will make spacing on the court more effective.

- Front court: The half-court area where the offensive team tries to score points.

- Back court: The half-court area where a team defends the ball and the basket.

- Baseline: The boundary line under the basket that extends to the sideline.

- Sideline: The boundary line that outlines the court on just the two long sides.

- The midcourt line separates the court into two halves.

- The offensive team has ten seconds to advance the ball past the midcourt line.

- After the offensive players are past midcourt, they must stay on that half of the court. If they step backward over the line, a backcourt violation occurs, and the other team gets possession of the ball.

- Many offensive plays start after the point guard crosses the midcourt line.

The standard basketball is orange or brown. Men's basketball uses a ball that is 29.5 inches in circumference. Women's basketball uses a ball that is 28.5 inches in circumference. After sixth grade, male grade school players switch to a men's ball from a women's ball. Younger players should use a junior ball, which is 27.5 inches in circumference. As they acquire better skills, they can move to a women's ball.

You must review specific areas of the court for your players. Baseline, sideline and midcourt make up the boundaries of the court. The key area, or "paint," as it's referred to, is important because many plays are run and shots are taken in this area.

Key Area

- A big rectangular area that extends from the foul line to the baseline is referred to as the "key." This area is usually painted a solid color, giving it the nickname "paint" or "lane."

- A three-second violation is called if a player stays in the key for three seconds or more. After the player leaves the key, he gets a new three second count every time he comes out of the key throughout the game.

Jump Ball Circle

- The jump ball circle is located at midcourt. A jump ball is used to start the game.

- Typically the jump ball is done by the tallest player on each team. These two players set up inside a smaller circle to get ready for the referee to toss the ball up into the air.

- The rest of the team circles around the jump ball area. A defensive player should stand a little behind the area in case the other team has a clear advantage of getting possession.

POSITIONS ON COURT

Although there are specific positions, players should be able to play anywhere on the court

Teams consist of five players on the court: Point guard, shooting guard, small forward, power forward, and center. In basketball terms, these positions are referred to by numbers. The point guard position is known as the "1," the shooting guard is the "2," the small forward is the "3," the power forward is the "4," and the center is the "5."

The "1," "2," and "3" positions are all interchangeable, as are the "4" and "5." All guards should be able to bring the ball up the court and shoot when the opportunity arises. The forward and the center players should be able to rebound and post up effectively to allow the ball to be passed to the inside for a higher-percentage shot.

Point Guard

- The point guard position is played by a player who has excellent ball-handling skills. Typically this is a team leader who has a sense for the game.

- Point guards are usually smaller in stature and are quick at dribbling and pushing the ball up the court.

- The point guard's job is to bring the ball up the court, set up plays, call out plays, and drive into lanes.

- The point guard also must be able to see the court well and get his teammates involved.

Guard

- The shooting guard position is played by a player with great shooting skills and scoring mentality.

- The shooting guard must have strong dribbling skills and be able to get his shots off quickly. Shooting guards should be able to shoot the ball after dribbling as well as catch and shoot.

- Guards also should be able to play aggressive defense and be able to pressure the ball handlers.

- Guards need to be able to shoot from the three-point line as well as have the ability to drive the basket.

Typically the shorter players on the team are the guards, and the taller players are the forwards. In recent years many teams have moved away from using height to determine position. The development and skill levels of players have improved, allowing many players to play different positions. Do not limit your players to playing one position. These young kids are still developing. You never know if a player is going to stop growing or continue to grow. Give players the opportunity to play all of the positions.

The focus of beginner players should be on skill work. They are too young to understand the positions. As a coach, you can put them into an area, but be flexible and allow everyone to play both inside and out. Ten- to twelve-year-olds have a better understanding of playing their position and what each role consists of. Thirteen- and fourteen-year-olds should be able to play their position properly at all times.

Forward

- There are two types of forwards: Small and power.

- The small forwards can play both inside and outside of the key area. These players are typically the most athletic and versatile. Small forwards aggressively attack by driving and cutting to the basket.

- Power forwards tend to be stronger and like to play in the post area. Power forwards play with their backs to the basket and rely on strength to get rebounds. Most of their points are scored from short-range jump shots and rebounds from missed shots.

Center

- The center is typically the tallest player and has a great sense of toughness and demands contact in the paint.

- This position gets a lot of rebounds and blocked shots. On offense this position receives the ball close to the basket.

- Centers serve as the first line of defense.

- Centers should have a soft shooting touch around the basket as well as the ability to go up strong to the basket.

REFEREE CALLS

Because the game is controlled by the referee, you need to understand what his or her signals mean

All teams must play by certain rules in order to assure a fair game. A referee blows a whistle to stop a play and then signals to indicate the violation. Typically there are two referees per game.

Beginner basketball might have a coach or parent refereeing to make corrections during a game. In these types of games, calls aren't made for every mistake. Instead, refs/coaches stop play, make corrections, and give the ball back to the player who committed the violation so the player can learn. If the same violation occurs twice, the ball then should go to the other team.

A referee typically positions himself or herself on the

Fouls

- A foul can happen when a player shoots. The fouled player shoots two shots from the foul line, and the shot is unguarded. The rest of the players line up outside the lane to prepare for a rebound.

- If a younger player cannot reach the basket from the foul line, allow the player to move into the lane area and take the foul shot.

- Players have ten seconds to shoot the ball.

- Remind players when there is a "one and one" situation so they can get a rebound on the missed shot.

Double Dribbling

- Younger players often commit the violation of double dribbling.

- Remind players that they have two options when they pick up the ball: Pass or shoot.

- You must stress the importance of the pivot foot.

Players must keep one foot down, preferably the left foot. This help the players pivot to find an open player when they pick up the ball.

- Remind players that they cannot dribble with both hands at one time.

baseline of the court. The other referee then runs down the court and positions himself on the sideline to watch the top of the key. Referees make calls quickly. At the time of a call, the referee blows the whistle, play stops, and the call is made. If a foul is committed, the referee will walk over to the score table and let the scorekeeper know which player committed the foul. Referees must be in good physical shape and must have extensive knowledge of the game.

Learning referee signals helps coaches, players, and parents understand the game better.

Traveling

- As a player moves up the court, he must continue dribbling. If he moves without dribbling, it is a traveling violation, also known as "walking."

- An exception to the rule comes when a player goes in for a layup. Two steps and a jump are allowed after the ball is picked up to make the shot.

- Beginner players often walk with the ball. This is a rule violation. Reinforce this rule; with repetition young players will understand.

Directional Signal

- It is of utmost importance that you understand the directional signal made by the referee so you know where your team shoots and who has possession.

- Beginner players have a hard time understanding which basket they shoot at; remind them throughout the game.

- Players have five seconds to inbound a ball to teammates. After a basket is scored, they should not give the referee the ball. They can take it out by themselves and continue playing.

- However, the ball must go to a ref when the whistle blows.

SCORING

Scoring a "basket" is also known as scoring a "field goal" or "hoop"

Basketball is played at a quick pace, and many points are scored. The first way to score is to make a basket. When a basket is made, points are given to your team. A basket can be worth two points or three points, depending on the distance of the shot. Three points are given when a player shoots behind the three-point line. All baskets made inside the three-point line are worth two points.

Another way to score is from the foul line. Each foul shot made is worth one point. When a foul occurs during a shot, the player is typically awarded two foul shots. If a player is shooting behind the three-point line and gets fouled, the player is awarded three foul shots.

When the opposing team has committed six to ten fouls, the player who is fouled shoots a "one and one." This means that he shoots one foul shot, and if he makes it, he gets to shoot another shot. If he misses, play is resumed.

Two-point Shots

- Shots taken near the basket generally have a better chance of going in.

- Players can score by driving to the basket for a layup or shooting a jump shot.

- Passing the ball to teammates, setting screens, and running fast breaks make for more options to score.

- Beginner players should practice only two-point shots. They will have more success shooting close-range shots. Otherwise, they will develop bad shooting habits, which could lead to poor technique.

Three-point Shots

- A basket made outside the three-point arc is worth three points.

- If a player gets fouled while shooting outside the three-point arc, the player shoots three foul shots.

- When shooting a three-point shot, a player must stay behind the line. If a foot is on the line before the player shoots, the shot will not count as a three-point basket. Instead, it will count as two points.

- Players are allowed to jump over the line after the ball is released from their hands.

A foul shot is also taken after a technical foul is committed. Technical fouls occur when there is unsportsmanlike conduct by a player or coach. This results in the opponent receiving two free throws as well as possession of the ball. Anyone who commits two technical fouls is removed from the game.

Foul Shots

- A foul is committed when a player makes illegal contact with an opposing player.

- Some fouls are also called "flagrant fouls," "intentional fouls," and "technical fouls."

- A charging foul occurs when an offensive player runs over a defensive player who has established position.

- Depending on the type of foul, a player will go to the foul line to shoot, or his team will receive possession of the ball.

"And One" Shots

- "And one" shots are an exciting part of the game.

- A player gets an "and one" shot after being fouled in the act of shooting. If the basket is made, the points will count, and one foul shot will be awarded also.

- The referee signals that the basket is good, and the player gets another opportunity to shoot from the foul line.

PRECAUTIONS & SAFETY

As the old saying goes, better safe than sorry; be sure your team is safe

You should have knowledge of basketball safety issues that you might encounter throughout the season. This knowledge, along with proper planning, will help you be prepared and ensure a safe basketball experience for all. As coach, you must provide your players with a safe environment for practices and games, provide first aid to players for minor injuries, and protect yourself from any liability issues related to player injuries.

Before the season starts, have players take a full physical exam to determine if they are in proper health to participate. Parents should also sign a consent form allowing their children to participate. You are responsible for checking the condition of the equipment and court before games and

KNACK COACHING YOUTH BASKETBALL

First-aid Kit

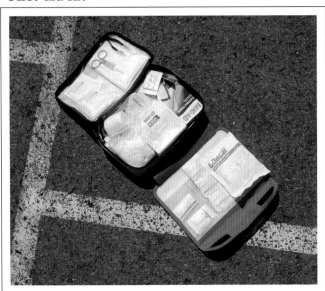

- A basic first-aid kit should have the supplies to treat an emergency. A small travel-size kit is enough to bring to games and practices.

- As players become older and advance to high school play, a full-time trainer is usually on staff.

- An assortment of supplies, such as gauze pads, scissors, bandages, instant cold packs, and gloves, is necessary in your first-aid kit.

Ice Packs

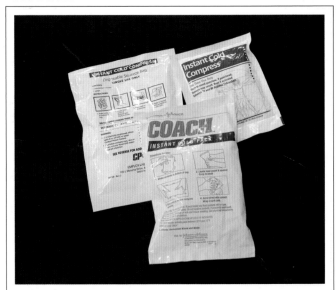

- You should carry breakable ice packs at all times. Breakable ice packs contain crushed ice crystals that, when broken up, turn cold.

- These instant cold packs stay cold for up to thirty minutes.

- Ice bags are not always available at a gym. So these instant cold packs will do the job. Cases of packs can be bought.

- Ice packs should be thrown out after use.

practices are played. You should properly condition your players to help prepare their bodies for games.

Adequate water breaks are a must during practices and games. Proper hydration must be incorporated into a practice plan; one or two water breaks will suffice.

In addition, supervision and drills appropriate for the age level will prevent many injuries. One of the most common ways in which smaller players are hurt is by being matched with teammates who are too big and strong for them. Match players with similar size and physical maturity.

Water/Sports Drinks

- Whether it's bottled water, sports drinks, or a water cooler, a necessary hydration station is a must at practices and games. Coaches must give adequate water breaks.

- Players typically bring their own drinks. However, a water fountain is available at all training facilities.

- Encourage kids to bring their own drinks to both practices and games.

- A water cooler can also be set up during games and practices.

Kneepads

- Kneepads are used to protect players' knees from bruises and floor burns.

- Younger players tend to fall more than older players because of lack of body strength.

- Kneepads come in different colors and padding. It is recommended that younger kids wear kneepads if they tend to fall a lot.

- Players should stay away from white bulky kneepads. These pads are cumbersome and tend to make a player look slow.

SAFETY

37

WEARING PROPER ATTIRE
Sneakers should have good traction to allow players to make quick stops and starts

Uniforms allow you to easily pick out members of your team. Uniforms also create an appearance of team unity. This sense of togetherness helps to create team chemistry. Members of a team who work together and produce results on court win together or lose together. Over the years uniforms have changed and become somewhat of a fashion statement.

However, standard uniform codes must be followed, including those that stipulate which numbers you can and cannot wear; certain numbers aren't allowed to be worn during game play.

A basic uniform consists of a loose-fitting jersey, usually sleeveless, loose-fitting shorts, usually at knee length or

Game Uniforms

- Game uniforms will be given to players to wear only for game play.

- Game uniforms are to be tucked into game shorts, and the proper number is to be worn.

- If a player chooses to wear a shirt underneath the jersey,

the shirt must be the same color as the jersey.

- School team and CYO players have to return uniforms at the end of the season.

- AAU teams and some travel teams purchase game uniforms and don't have to return them.

Game Uniforms for Younger Players

- Game uniforms for younger players and recreation league players usually consist of a T-shirt and a player's choice of shorts.

- A logo of some sort will be on the front of the T-shirt, with the player's number on back. Players will be given the T-shirt to keep as part of

signing up for the recreation department.

- Some leagues have reversible jerseys or mesh lightweight jerseys.

- If a team is financially stretched, a uniform can be any type of shirt as long as a number is on the back.

slightly above, and well-fitting shoes with strong ankle support. Each part of the uniform is important and serves its purpose.

Uniforms allow you to easily identify teammates and see each player's number, which is good for discerning who fouled or scored points. The loose-fitting uniform also allows for movement. The loose-fitting nature of uniforms allows players to move quickly and without hindrance. Tight uniforms would hinder movement and flexibility and become a hassle.

Uniforms are also used to protect players. The proper shoes protect players from an ankle injury, and proper-fitting uniforms prevent players from catching on clothing that is too big.

Basketball shoes, perhaps the most important piece of the uniform, come in a variety of brands and colors. Some teams agree to buy the same color or type of sneakers, whereas other teams don't. Players should break in their sneakers well before wearing them in a game. Otherwise, blisters can occur and result in players having to leave a game.

Practice Attire

- The choice of practice attire will be up to each player. Loose-fitting T-shirts and shorts are recommended.

- Sweatpants are also recommended in the winter months.

- Some school teams provide players with practice gear.

Practice gear consists of a reversible jersey, shorts, and T-shirt.

- Reversible jerseys are a good idea to purchase for practice because players don't have to share pinnies and can use their jerseys in scrimmages.

Sneakers

- Basketball sneakers are sold at all sporting goods stores. A comfortable mid- to high-top sneaker is recommended for solid ankle support.

- Basketball sneakers are often made of light materials but still have support around the ankles.

- Sneakers come in a variety of colors and styles. I recommend having players buy a boy's basketball sneaker. There are few girls-only basketball shoes.

- Each player will decide which shoe he likes best and which fits best.

CONDITIONING: 6–9-YEAR-OLDS
Kids don't play to get in shape; they get in shape to play

Conditioning in this age group is unnecessary because kids are always running around anyway, and they enjoy playing. Coaches need to keep it fun and not worry about conditioning. When kids are tired, they will simply slow down and when ready, they will pick up their speed again. Do not force kids to do running drills. Keep it fun and light, and kids will respond better.

At this time of development stretching can be taught. Kids are flexible, so stretching won't make too much of a difference, but it will prepare the kids for later in their development when they will have to stretch. Warm-up drills, such as doing jumping jacks or jogging in place, should be part of the stretching routine. When kids do running drills, a basketball should be dribbled to teach kids how to run and dribble at the same time.

Stretching routines should be simple and done correctly.

Stretching

- Stretching takes place after warm-ups.

- A light, short stretch is recommended for players in this age category. Younger players are flexible and don't require much stretching.

- Arm stretches can be done first and then basic leg touches.

- Finish by having players sit on the ground and do a groin stretch or a sit-and-reach stretch. After stretching is done, explain to players what will happen in practice. At this time you will have their attention.

Jumping Jacks

- Jumping jacks are a good exercise for younger players to develop coordination and conditioning.

- Jumping jacks can be used as a warm-up before stretching. Or they can be used as a penalty when doing competitive drills.

- They are also useful in relay races when you want to add something extra to the end of the races.

- Jumping jacks work on full body conditioning.

Make sure players do not bounce up and down while stretching and do not stretch to the point of pain. Remind players to breathe. Younger players tend to hold their breath. The point of stretching is to loosen the muscles and increase flexibility. A cool-down at the end of practice is a good idea; try walking around the court. At this time important points about practice can be made and encouragement given.

Riverbank

- Riverbank is a fun coordination game. Play it at the beginning of practice when players are most attentive.

- Players stand around the court, outside of the sideline and baseline. When you yell "River," players must jump over the line into the river (the inside of the court). When you yell "Bank," they must jump backward onto the banks (the outside of the court).

- If a player jumps on the line, fumbles, or loses his balance, he is out. Play until one player is left standing.

Pivoting without a Ball

- Another good warm-up drill to teach players how to pivot is to have them pivot without a ball.

- Players scatter around the court with a pretend ball in their hands. When the whistle blows, players run around the court in any direction.

- When the whistle blows again, all players stop and pivot. Players continue to pivot until the whistle blows again. Then they continue running.

- To pivot, hold the left foot down and move the right foot. Left-handed players tend to pivot on the left foot.

SAFETY

CONDITIONING: 10–12-YEAR-OLDS

Athletes must do each exercise carefully; speed is not important

The game of basketball requires running. If players can't run, they can't play. It's as simple as that. Player's must get into shape to play. The worst losses come when an opposing team outruns or is in better shape than your team. Coaches and players have full control over how conditioned they are. The toughest team on the court is the team that can last the longest. If players are not properly conditioned, then no matter how skilled they are, they won't be able to utilize their

skills very long in the game. Properly conditioned teams tend to be faster, stronger, and better overall.

Before conditioning or stretching, have your team warm up by jogging or doing jumping jacks. After your players are warmed up, stretching (for a total of ten minutes) should take place. Several different stretches can be performed every day in practice to ensure that all body parts are stretched.

Upper-body stretches to keep arms limber should consist

Arm Stretches

- Arm stretching is important to loosen muscles that will be used after practice starts.

- Arm circles in both big and small movements and reversed directions are ideal.

- Stretch the arm across the body and pull it into the chest with the other arm.

- Use a partner to stand behind a player and pull the arm in a controlled manner.

- Flex the wrist to loosen the wrist muscles.

Leg Stretches

- Stretching the legs is important because the legs get a good deal of use. Proper stretching must take place to avoid pulled muscles and cramping.

- Hamstring muscles need the most stretching.

- The groin area needs to be

stretched as well.

- Calf muscles tend to cramp up and become sore; toe raises will take care of the calf muscles.

- Encourage players to stretch on their own if they are extra sore.

of arm circles, stretching arms across the body and pulling the elbows down behind the head. After the upper body the groin and hamstring areas must be stretched. The hamstring area needs the most stretching due to the constant squatting in this sport. Calf muscles should also be stretched. Each stretch should be held for ten seconds.

Sprints

- After warm-ups and stretches, players need to get into intense game speed.

- Have them sprint up and down court to warm up their bodies.

- Try this: Two lines of players line up on the baseline.

Blow the whistle; the first two people take off in an all-out sprint to the opposite three-point line. When they reach the three-point line, they back pedal off the court with their hands over their heads.

- Repeat the process with all players.

Pivoting with a Ball

- Pivoting with a ball is a drill that works on pivoting, conditioning, and dribbling.

- Players scatter around the court, dribbling a ball. Blow the whistle to indicate to players to start. Players dribble around making different moves. When you blow the whistle again,

players stop, pick up the ball, and begin to pivot.

- Players must keep their heads up and pay attention to where they are going. Encourage players to stay lower when pivoting and to hold the ball tightly.

SAFETY

CONDITIONING: 13–14-YEAR-OLDS

Players should work on quickness, agility, hand-eye coordination, and physical conditioning

Basketball is both an aerobic and anaerobic sport. Players need to maintain high-level conditioning to play an entire game. At the same time, players use bursts of speed to quickly get down the court or to blow by a defender. Players need to condition themselves to do both. Because basketball players use their entire body, players especially need to work on their core. The core—also known as the "abdominal area"—needs to be strong because of the amount of contact that goes on throughout a game. The stronger the player is, the better off he will be. Strong players will be able to position themselves to grab rebounds, establish a good defense stance, and drive to the basket hard.

Endurance Runs

- Endurance should be worked on during the preseason and the first weeks of practice.

- Players line up on the sideline. Players begin to jog together in a line. When you blow the whistle, the last person in line sprints to the front of the line. This process is repeated until every player gets a chance to lead the line.

- Run this drill for ten minutes.

Leg Stretches

- Strengthening legs and developing quick feet are essential in basketball.

- High knees and butt kicks develop strength. Grapevines develop agility and quick feet.

- Defensive slides develop strong quads and hamstrings. And calf muscles can be developed by jumping rope.

- Basketball players should have a lean, muscular look. Players shouldn't try to bulk up too much. Remember that basketball is a combination of speed, agility, and strength.

Conditioning should be maintained throughout the season. Preseason conditioning will require more intense workouts to prepare for the upcoming season. Jump ropes, line jumps, suicides, 17s, push-ups and sit-ups, and 3-mile runs all should be done during the preseason. During the actual season, players should maintain that high-level intensity, but focus is more on skill work along with conditioning. Drills should consist of defensive slides, full-court transition drills, shooting drills, and live rebounding drills.

As the season progresses and more games are played, the focus turns to execution of plays and skill work. At this time conditioning still needs to be maintained. Conditioning can be maintained by doing live scrimmaging and three-on-three and one-on-one drills.

Because teams have limited practice time, encourage players to do skill work on their own. If it's too cold outside for players to practice, use several basketball facilities around the area that allow players to rent a basket. Also encourage players to show up early to practice or stay after to get in more shooting practice.

Foot Slides

- Defensive footwork is key to playing good defense.

- Coaches need to develop players' footwork through a series of quick agility drills.

- Players will spread out on half the court. Point in the direction you want players to slide.

- Give different signals for players to do various skills.

- Fast feet is a drill in which players tap their feet in place in a fast manner. You can also have players jump up and down, simulating grabbing for a rebound. Various footwork drills can be done at this time.

Suicides

- Suicides, or line sprints, are simply sprints to a certain line and back to the baseline. When players reach a line, they touch it with their hand and run back.

- A typical suicide is from the baseline to the foul line and back, to the half court and back, and to the opposite foul line and back.

- Suicides also can be timed and done while dribbling a basketball.

- Double suicides double up on the same drill.

CONDITIONING
No coach should start a game with poorly conditioned players

It is best to run a lot of conditioning drills early in the season. Players typically come into the season out of shape. Use as many conditioning drills as possible to get the players into shape. Each practice should consist of a fair amount of conditioning, but remember that when players go hard each drill and run from drill to drill, they will be in good shape. Don't work players into the ground, but let them know why conditioning is important.

Conditioning youth players requires much more than just running and sprinting. Basketball is a game of movement; however, coaches tend to ignore movement skills and focus on basketball-specific drills. Nothing is more important than teaching players to move correctly. Teach them how to run, how to slide, and how to jump.

From the youth level up through seventh and eighth grades, time spent on conditioning drills should be limited

Line Conditioning for Younger Players

- Use the outside boundaries of the full court for this drill.

- Have players stand in one line. Call out a type of run for the players to do. For example, tell players to jog around two laps. The next commands go as follows: Skip around the court. Walk around the court with your hands over your head.

- Be creative, but don't tire players out too much.

Line Jumps

- At the middle-aged level, line jumps are useful for conditioning, strength, and coordination.

- Have players pick a line anywhere on court and stand to the side of the line.

- Players will jump side to side over the line in thirty-second intervals. Their hands will be over their heads as they jump.

- Then switch. Have players jump front to back and then jump in a box formation, hitting all four corners. They can also jump on one foot.

to ten minutes in the beginning of practice. Players this age naturally run around and don't tire easy. They are kids, and kids run around. Several individual basic conditioning drills can be done using the full court. Conditioning drills such as jogging, skipping, sliding, and butt kicks. Players can then form a circle and stretch after these drills are done.

Group warm-up drills should take place after individual conditioning drills. These drills can be broken down into dribbling, pivoting, passing, and jumping. The drills involve the team as a whole. Don't forget to incorporate transition drills. Players love the two-on-one, the three-on-two, and eleven man fast break drills. Alternate drill work on conditioning skills and both offense and defense. Start the season with easier drills, increasing in difficulty as the season progresses.

Chase Layups

- Here players line up equally on opposite baselines with three basketballs per line. Players throw the ball to you while you stand at the elbow of the foul line.

- You will throw the ball down court aiming for the opposite foul line. The player takes off and catches up to the ball to dribble in for a layup.

- Don't throw the ball too far out of the player's reach.

- Remind players to throw the ball to you only when you are looking.

Two-minute Layups

- The two-minute layup drill is used to see how many layups players can make in two minutes as a team.

- Set a goal for your players, such as making thirty layups. Set the goal tailored to your team.

- This layup is done with players dribbling the length of the floor. The next player in line can't start until the person in front of him reaches the first foul line.

- Have managers count baskets made.

47

PRACTICE WARM-UPS
Fundamentals are the essence of basketball skills

Train your players to practice hard so they can perform in the game. Drills and warm-ups break down the various parts of the game into the basics so players can systematically build their skills. After players warm up with conditioning drills and stretching, it's time to put a ball into their hands. Starting practice with ball-handling drills is ideal to get players to move their hands. Dribbling drills can be done both stationary and full court. You might not have enough basketballs for every kid to do stationary ball handling, so go into dribble lines. Keep in mind that these drills should not last more than ten to fifteen minutes at a time.

Make use of your gym; if you have six available baskets, use them. Assign partners to each basket to work on individual shooting and partner shooting. You can get a lot accomplished by breaking kids into groups. Select drills that help teach individual and team fundamental drills. Incorporate

Running Passes

- Separate players in two equal lines behind cones.

- One line is in one corner of the court, and the other is in the opposite corner.

- Have alternate players from each line run out. Player A runs to the jump ball circle area with a ball. Player A passes to player B, who passes to player C, and so forth.

- Switch up passes. All players must stay to the right and run around the opposite cone to turn around and continue the drill.

Five-spot Shooting

- Five-spot shooting allows players to take a lot of shots during a short period of time and from different spots on the floor.

- The five spots are two corners, two wings, and the foul line.

- Two to three players line up in the corner. All players have basketballs. Player A tosses the ball to them and shoots; player B does the same.

- After every player shoots the ball five times from a spot, the players move together to the next spot.

drills in a progression; start off basic and then progress into more advanced drills.

Younger players need repetition. Doing the same drills is fine until your team understands and is ready for more advanced drills. Don't forget to incorporate shooting free throws in between drills. Players will be able to shoot foul shots under game-like conditions.

Endurance Run

- Players line up on the sideline and jog around the outside of the court. Blow your whistle to let the last player know he must sprint to the front of the line.

- Players can run on the outside or inside of the pack of players.

- Continue to blow your whistle until all players get to the front of the line.

- This drill both conditions and teaches sprinting.

Defensive Closing Out Drill

- Players get in groups of three.

- One player will be in the middle with the ball as the defensive player, the other two are opposite each other.

- The middle player passes the ball to either player and runs

- to play defense by closing out toward that player.

- Once the defense is successful, the person with the ball dribbles back to the middle, jump stops, and throws ball to the opposite player. He then closes out toward the other player. Drill continues.

LAYUPS

Practice drills need to support a coach's practice plan

For youth players you want to focus on long-term development, so what better way to start than with layups? Layups should be the first shooting drills taught. Have players practice lots of layups with both hands. Your goal should be to get all players to make layups with their left and right hands equally well.

Start players really close to the basket with no dribble. Have a coach at the basket talking each player through the steps.

On the right side the coach says, "Right, left jump." Make sure each player jumps toward the basket. Players should jump off their left foot and lift up their right leg to their chest. Left-side layups are the opposite. If players have a hard time shooting with their left hand, encourage them to dribble with the left hand and do the proper footwork. They can shoot with the right hand until they are ready to reach the basket with the left hand.

One-line Layups

- All players start in one line behind the three-point line.

- The first player dribbles in for a layup, gets the rebound, and gives the ball to the next player in line.

- As the drill progresses, move the line back to half court.

- This drill helps young players to get their own rebounds and dribble back to give to the next player. It also forces players to develop three skills: Shoot, dribble, and rebound.

Two-line Layups

- In this drill two lines are formed at half court opposite each other. One line has two basketballs.

- As player A from the shooting line runs in for a layup, the player from the rebounding line runs in as well. Player A shoots a layup and continues to run, while the other player jumps up, grabs the rebound, and dribbles to the shooting line.

- Remind players not to dribble up the middle after rebounds; they must dribble on the outside to get to the other line.

Middle-aged kids with a year or two of basketball skills can do half-court and full-court layups. At this age layups should become second nature. Add backdoor cuts to layups. Introduce different layups, such as power and reverse. Right- and left-hand layups should be done correctly and made on a consistent basis.

Advanced players should incorporate a dribble move into a layup. They should be able to get to the basket in limited dribbles. Players at this age should have no problem taking one dribble from the three-point line to make a layup. They should be able to get down the court in five dribbles to perform a layup. Spend time doing layups within drills at this age level.

Full-court Layups

- Players line up in opposite lines in the corner of the baseline. Each dribbles to half court, makes a dribble move, and then dribbles in for a layup on the opposite end of the court.

- Players then get back in line and reverse the drill on the other half of the court.

- The drill can last ten minutes. Then switch sides of the court and switch to dribble moves.

- Players in line should not go until the previous player gets to half court.

Loop Layups

- Here players start in two lines under the basket, one basketball in each line. One line has the second player holding the ball. Player A from that line loops in the lane to the opposite side and receives the ball from player B in the opposite line.

- Player B shoots a power layup, gets the rebound, and gives the ball to the player waiting on the same side the layup was taken.

- Player A then loops behind player B and gets the ball from the opposite side to do a power layup.

PASSING
Don't overlook this fundamental skill

Basketball is a team sport. When the ball moves and everyone gets involved, scoring will come quite easily. Passing skills are sometimes overlooked. Many drills are done on the move with full-court passing. Others are done as basic half-court drills, such as partner passing, star passing, monkey in the middle, drive and dish, and four corners. Passing drills are important at the youth level to let players get familiar with their teammates, get used to catching the ball, and understand team concepts.

When you introduce passing at the beginner level, start with three basic passes: Chest, bounce, and overhead. At times players may be afraid of the ball. Teach them to catch with their hands and not with their chest. Partner passing is a great warm-up drill to do. It gets players passing correctly and gets them familiar with different players on the team.

At the intermediate and advanced levels, passing drills

Circle Passing

- This is a great drill for younger players both to learn to pass and to learn teammates' names.

- All players make a big circle around the jump ball area. One player stands in the middle and calls out a teammate's name before passing to him. The teammate passes back. This middle player then passes around the circle to every other player. After all players touch the ball, a new person comes to the middle.

- Change passes and remind players to call out names.

Star Passing

- Here five players—two wing, two corner players, and one center—start in a star pattern. The rest of the team lines up under the basket. Player A passes the ball to player B in the right wing, then follows the pass to the right. Player B passes to the corner, follows the pass. The corner passes to the opposite corner, follows pass. The corner passes to the opposite wing, who cuts to the basket for a layup.

- There should now be a player in all four spots. Drill continues. Remind players to stay to the right when they pass, and then to the left when you switch sides.

should be done within a drill. Don't waste time with basic partner passing. Instead, have players pass basketballs into a shot, pass balls while players move their feet quickly in a semicircle, or practice passing by playing three-on-three with no dribbles. Practice passing under pressure as well as breaking a press and moving to an open spot.

Younger players have a tendency to lob the ball and not throw a crisp, hard pass. Remind them they must reach the other person. Younger players also tend to wait for the ball. Instead, players should jump to the pass when receiving it.

Jumping to the ball and having a wide base allow players to maneuver more.

Fast Feet Passing

- Here one player has the ball. Five other players gather around in a semicircle formation.

- All players fast feet on the floor. The player in the middle throws the ball to the first player in the semicircle. That player throws back. Middle player throws

to the next player, who then throws back. This continues to all players. Then the middle player becomes part of the semicircle, and a new player comes into the middle.

- All players must do fast feet throughout the drill. Passes can be changed.

Four-corner Passing

- Players form four lines of three players each to make a square formation around the key.

- One ball starts in one line, the other starts in line diagonal to them. Player with ball passes in line directly in front, gets ball back, and then passes right back to that player. Player goes to end of line. The player that receives ball then passes to the line to the right. This continues to form a square pattern of passing.

- The first pass should be a hard pass, then followed by a close, soft touch pass back and forth.

- Two balls are used at once. Players must pay attention and rotate in the same direction.

- After a few minutes, switch directions.

53

DEFENSIVE SLIDES

Good offense wins games, but great defense wins championships

When it comes to defense, everyone on the team has to play well. One weak link will cause the entire defense to break down. Playing good defense requires hustle, hard work, and proper footwork. Defensive skills are easy to learn, and everyone can learn to become a good defender.

Practicing drills that involve defensive slides can be used to teach proper footwork and proper stance. Start with the basics; explain the defensive stance, then incorporate drills that make players have to guard someone. Drills require players to stay low and work on leg strength and conditioning.

Several drills can be run during warm-ups. At the beginning of practice, teach proper defensive skills and conditioning at the same time. Defensive drills can be done in various ways.

Break defense down into two parts: individual defense and team defense. Individual defense drills will focus on proper footwork, sliding, and staying lower in front of who the

Basic Slides

- Players spread out on half of the court, about one arm's length away from each other. Call out, "Defense." Players then slap the floor, yell "Defense," and get into a proper defensive stance.

- Yell out commands for players to follow, such as "Side to side" or "Back and forth."

- Players can also jump up into the air while yelling "Rebound." Or players can stutter their feet while turning side to front to side again.

- After ninety seconds, give players a rest before continuing.

Guarding Dribbler

- Here players partner up with another player of equal ability to go head to head. Player A is on defense, player B on offense.

- Player B goes half speed and changes direction in a zigzag manner. Player B will work on his defensive stance, sliding, and keep-ing eyes on the dribbler's stomach area.

- Players will zigzag to the end of the court, then switch offense to defense.

- A more advanced drill requires players to switch to full speed after they hit half court.

player is guarding. Individual defense also involves denying the player the ball while seeing the ball at all times. Team defense requires players to talk to each other on court, play help defense, and close gaps when necessary. Take time when explaining team defense and stop play when a player is out of position until they understand how to move when the ball is rotated.

Defense Recovery

- Two lines form on the base-line, one 5 feet in front of the other. The first two players in each line are ready to run with knees bent. Toss the ball to the player who is in the closer line.

- After catching the ball, the player dribbles full speed to the opposite end to shoot

a layup. At the same time the player in the other line sprints down court to catch the offensive player.

- The defensive player tries to sprint in front of the offensive player and then turns in front of him to recover and continue to play defense.

Full-court Slides

- Players line up in two lines on opposite corners of the baseline.

- The first player slides to the elbow, then to half court to the other elbow, then to the baseline.

- When the player reaches the baseline, he does an all-

out sprint down the sideline to get back into line.

- Remind players to open up when they reach their marks and not turn their backs. They should face the same way the entire time.

- Have every player go three times through the line.

GAME WARM-UP DRILLS

Have a system to determine which drills players run before games

Every team needs adequate warm-up before a game. Warm-up drills are the perfect way to get team members working together, warmed up, and focused on the game. Game warm-up drills usually involve light running, shooting, and passing. These drills are not tiring, but they do prepare the muscles for the game. Warm-ups give players a chance to get their heads into the game and to focus on the task ahead.

Warm-up drills should not last more than twenty minutes.

Ten minutes is the average amount of time. To maximize your time, keep drills simple and quick. Remember that you're not trying to tire out your players. End warm-ups with foul shots and have players come into a huddle with one minute remaining on the clock.

Some gyms play music during warm-ups. Players love it because they get excited and motivated. Some teams like to clap and slap high fives throughout warm-ups. Many teams

Basic Shooting Lines

- Here two lines form at half court (shooting, rebounding) with two balls in the shooting line.

- The first player dribbles to the elbow and shoots the ball. A player from the rebounding line runs in at the same time and gets the rebound.

- The rebounding player dribbles along the outside and gives the ball to the shooting line.

- Players then switch lines. Switch sides after a few minutes. Players also can do a dribble move and then pull up to shoot.

Roll Out to Layup

- Two lines form on the baseline across the key with two balls in one line. The player with the ball rolls it out to the elbow in a controlled roll. The player in the other line simultaneously runs to the elbow without ball.

- Both players turn inward. The player without the ball

cuts to the basket, while the other picks up the ball and bounce passes to the player cutting.

- That player shoots, while the passer gets the rebound and switches lines.

follow the same drills. Older teams often employ the use of a captain to lead warm-ups, telling other players when to switch sides and drills. Younger teams need coaches and assistant coaches on court during warm-ups to provide guidance and help rebound. Players should stretch on their own, often before game warm-ups.

Dribble Pass Layup

- Two lines form on the base-line, one with basketballs, the other without. Both lines face half court.

- The first player dribbles up to half court, while the other player without the ball runs to half court at the same time. When they reach half court, they turn.

The player with the ball dribbles to the elbow, while the other runs in for a layup. The player with the ball bounce passes to the other, who shoots the layup, gets the rebound, and switches lines.

Pass to Shot

- Players make one line in the corner with two balls. One player is at the top of the key, and one player is in the opposite corner.

- The first player in line in the corner (A) passes to the player at the top of the key (B) and then follows the pass. Player B passes to

player C, who then shoots the ball. Player B follows his pass. Player C gets the rebound and goes into line in corner. This pattern continues.

- Start with regular jump shots and then move back to three-point shots.

WARM-UP DRILLS

TECHNIQUE & FORM
Be sure that kids practice under game-like conditions

The most popular skill practiced in the game of basketball is shooting. Whether they practice individually or as a team, players must be able to shoot the ball correctly. Often younger players practice the wrong technique because they shoot out of range. Players must practice game-like shots in order to become successful shooters. A player will not get better just by "shooting around" at a lazy pace. Shooting for a solid hour or hour and a half under game-like

conditions with full speed is ideal. Anything more than that is too much, and anything less than full speed may not be enough.

Players master their shots through repetition and practice. Shooting drills should focus on timing, accuracy, and range. Coaches should conduct many shooting drills in practice. These drills build team strength and success. Coaches and players on all levels are always trying to

Basic Form

- Good shooters believe that every ball will go in.

- The shooting arm should be at a 90-degree angle, slightly off to the side. The elbow should be straight and not tucked into the waist.

- The "Y" between the thumb

and the index finger of the shooting hand ensures proper placing of the ball. This hand is placed in the middle of the ball.

- The non-shooting hand is on the side of the ball. This hand has no other function in the shot other than to hold the ball, palm facing inward.

Follow-through

- Players should follow through all shots. A follow-through should be a quick snap of the wrist in the shape of a goose neck.

- The follow-through should be held for two seconds after the ball is released from the hand.

- Before the ball is released, the player should bend the hand back so the wrinkle on the back of the wrist can be seen.

- Players should not place the ball in the palm of the hand or on the fingertips. The ball should rest slightly off of the palm on the finger pads.

improve their shooting. By far the best shooting way to perfect technique is form shooting. All players must master technique in order to become better shooters.

Balance

- Legs should be shoulder width apart. Shoulders should be square to the basket at all times when shooting.

- The strength of the shot comes from the legs, not arm strength.

- Players should have knees bent at all times and jump in a up and down manner.

- Shooting technique does not change with more range. The only thing that changes is the amount of leg strength used.

Rotation of the Ball

- The ball is released when a shooter is on her way up (in the legs).

- Her eyes should remain focused on the front of the rim. They should not follow the flight of the ball.

- Jump shots in basketball, with the exception of foul shots, cannot be aimed. Players need to sight the basket and rely on use of proper form.

- The basketball should have a back spin. Releasing the ball by the fingertips gives the ball a spin.

LAYUPS

The easiest and most popular shot in basketball should be the first one players learn

Layups are the most basic shot in basketball and the first shot players learn. Layups are made by shooting the ball off the backboard. Players aim at the square above the basket to ensure the shot goes in. When teaching young players how to do layups, start with the power layup. Power layups require less foot work, which makes it easier for the beginner player to shoot the correct way off of the backboard. Middle-aged players will be able to do layups easily after this basic technique is mastered. More advanced players will develop other ways to do layups, such as reverse, underhand, and hook.

Layups should eventually be taught at full speed and performed at an angle to the basket. Players can remember to

Power Layups for Younger Kids

- Teach younger players to aim for the square on the backboard.

- Have players take a step inside the box to shoot a power layup. The box is too far away for them otherwise, and it then becomes a jump shot.

- Players should start at the three-point line, dribble past the box, stop square with feet and shoulders to the basket, and jump off of both feet.

Regular Layups

- Teach kids to step right-left-jump on the right side and left-right-jump on the left side. They can do this footwork as a group up the court several times. Practice footwork without the ball before doing the actual layup.

- Teaching layups using a wall helps establish proper footwork and helps players to concentrate on footwork rather than making baskets.

- Have players dribble in for a layup from three-point arc.

- Remind players not to stop while dribbling but rather to continue to lay the ball up to the backboard.

jump by taking a last step after the box and jumping toward the basket.

When a player shoots a layup on the right side of the basket, the right leg should be lifted up toward the chest. The same goes for the left side. The left leg lifts toward the chest. Emphasis should be placed on dribbling with the left hand and the left side. Right-handed younger players will have difficulty shooting with their left hand. Allow them to shoot with the right hand until they get strong enough to shoot with the left.

Jump Stop Power Layup

- When a player does a jump stop before shooting a power layup, he should make sure the jump stop is not a hard jump. Injury can occur if a player jumps too hard.

- Instead a jump stop should be a controlled jump right before the shot.

- After the player comes to a jump stop, he must square his shoulders to the basket and jump again toward the basket.

- He should softly shoot the ball off the backboard but jump in a powerful manner.

Reverse Layup

- Reverse layups should be done by advanced players only and are best performed when a player is coming from close behind the basket.

- Here are the mechanics for the shot: Lean head back to sight basket, do not turn the head around.

- Do not drop the ball below the waist to shoot. Use a hook-like shot from the chest up with a flick of the wrist off of the backboard.

- Lift the right or left leg, depending on the side, the same way players lift their leg up for regular layups.

61

JUMP SHOTS

To keep it simple, have your players practice from all areas of the court

Shooting position begins when a player is set in an athletic stance with the knees bent and the hands ready to receive the ball. Shooting is done in one quick motion in which the player jumps and releases the ball in a follow-through manner. Hands should already be set to bring the ball up into the shooting pocket, and the body should be squared to the

basket. Eyes should focus on the front of the rim. Shoulders should also be squared to the basket slightly ahead of the hips. The ball will be caught just below the chin. The ball should not be in front of the face, blocking the view of the basket. And the ball should not drop below the waist, resulting in a shot that is too long and will be blocked.

Two-handed Shot

- Beginner players should shoot the ball with both hands. Hands are placed on both sides of the ball, slightly underneath.

- Follow-through is a must after players take the shot.

- Remind players to always square their feet and shoulders to the basket. They should have knees bent to get power from the legs, avoid throwing the body into the shot, and avoid kicking their legs.

- If younger players can't reach the basket, let them use a junior ball.

Jump Shot

- Players ten to twelve years of age should learn to shoot with one hand.

- Form shooting drills must be done to reinforce proper form.

- Practice all shots inside the key; do not go out to a three-point range.

- Both girls and boys at this age will use the women's ball to shoot.

- Knees should be bent, hand ready to catch ball, once ball is caught player will bring ball to shooting pocket jump and shoot jump shot.

Younger players tend to shoot from their waist to get strength. This position must be corrected right away. It's important to release the ball at the peak of the jump shot. When a player jumps to shoot, the feet should land in the same spot he jumped from. Players often jump forward, which throws off their shot. Others jump back or move to the side, which results in a loss of power. When shooting the ball, players should not drop the nonshooting hand; dropping the hand will cause the body to turn. The nonshooting hand does not move as the palm always faces inward.

Form Shooting

- Form shooting works on proper shooting technique. This drill is done close to the basket and only swish shots should be made.

- Make sure that the follow-through ends in a goose neck shape with the hand and that the ball rotates properly.

- Before players take the shot, fix the ball so the seams go across the ball, not up and down. This allows players to see the proper rotation as the ball successfully comes off the finger tips.

- The non-shooting hand is off the ball but still up by the ball. See picture above.

Rules for Form Shooting

- When a player is form shooting, he must not jump; he must finish on his toes.

- The ball is in the shooting hand with the elbow bent in a 90-degree angle, away from the chest.

- The opposite hand should be up but off the ball.

- The knees should be bent, feet shoulder width apart.

- Players should not bring the ball down to shoot. Rather, with the legs already bent, they should go straight up from the shooting pocket.

- Players should hold the follow-through for two seconds.

OFF THE DRIBBLE

These shots give players many opportunities to score

When a player shoots the ball off the dribble, several events must occur before bringing the ball into the shooting pocket. First, proper foot work is extremely important. If a player is right-handed, as most players are, he must step into the shot with the left foot first and then the right foot, shoulder width apart. The player's feet must be even.

The opposite is true for a left-handed player. The ball is dribbled not on the side but rather in front. The dribble in front

should be a hard, fast dribble to get the ball quickly into the shooting pocket. Reaching back for the basketball will result in a slow release and give the defense time to get in front of the shooter. Keep in mind that dribbling in front of the defender can result in the basketball being stolen.

Players who dribble off a screen or at an angle must be able to stop with the proper foot. The simplest way to teach which foot to step with is to tell players to step with the foot closest

Angle Shots

- Angle shots require proper footwork. Practicing these types of shots allows players to work on squaring to the basket. Stepping with the inside pivot foot allows for a quicker turn.

- Angle shots can start in the middle of the court and drive to the elbows for a pull-up jump shot. Work on both right and left sides.

- Dribbling from wing to corner also allows players to develop squaring to the basket.

Dribbling off Screen

- "Dribbling off screen" means player must rub one side of the shoulder of the person setting the screen so the defensive player doesn't get through.

- When a defensive player goes below the screen, the dribbler has the opportunity to shoot a jump shot.

- When a defensive player gets stopped by the screener trying to get over the screen, this signals the offensive player to drive toward the basket. The defensive player runs behind the offensive player, giving the offensive player the advantage.

to the basket first. This technique is called a "change of the pivot foot." If a player is having a difficult time understanding this concept and finds himself walking, have the player always step with his left foot first. Again, this will be opposite for a left-handed player.

Advanced players should learn how to change pivot feet. It makes shooting a lot quicker and gives players the opportunity to do more things with the ball. Younger players should be taught to take a one-two step, or a left-right step, when dribbling into the shot.

Dribble Pull-ups

- Have players dribble full speed into a shot with eyes up, looking at the basket.

- Players should never jump stop before shooting a jump shot. Injury will take place due to the amount of pressure on the knees. Players should take baby steps to slow down before stepping into the shot.

- Pull-up shots can be taken anywhere on the court.

- Players should start in a triple threat position; their first dribble should be a long step with the ball pushed out. This allows the player to step past the defender.

Step Back

- Step-back moves are used by more advanced players to avoid trapping situations. Players should lean the body forward to get defenders to go backward. The offensive player then hops back with both feet.

- Another variation is to lean with one foot and then step back with the opposite foot. Legs must be bent at all times.

- Step-back moves can be performed without picking up the ball. To avoid being trapped or getting stuck in a corner, players can dribble in a backward motion.

CATCH & SHOOT

All players love shooting, but to be good at it, they must work consistently

Whether it's a pass coming off the screen, a wide open shot, or a skip pass, players need to be ready to quickly catch and shoot the basketball. That is, their feet must be squared to the basket, the body bent, and hands in the ready position. Open players should call for a ball or raise their hands so the passer can see them.

Ready hands are critical in catching and shooting the ball. When the ball is passed to the shooter, she then must step into the pass. The step should be a one-two step to the basket but often varies depending on the shot. For example, when coming off a screen, a player can try a one-two step to turn the body. When catching the ball from a stationary

Ready to Shoot

- Any sport requires players to be in an athletic stance at all times during the course of the practice or game.

- Because strength is needed from the legs to shoot the ball, players must have accurate body positioning and stance at all times.

Foot Position

- When shooting, players must have their feet pointed toward the basket, regardless of whether players come off a screen, make a move, or dribble straight in.

- Younger players tend to twist their bodies in the air during their shot.

- Have players hold their position after their shot and freeze. This allows them to see exactly the direction in which their feet are pointed.

- Repeating this process will force players to point their feet in the correct manner.

spot, a small step is efficient. And taking a long step slows up the shot.

When a player spots up—which means to wait to receive the ball in a ready position in a certain spot on the floor—to shoot with a step pass, no step is required. Typically the ball comes over the head, and the player gets his feet set under the ball to receive it. When a player comes off a screen to shoot, he must be shoulder to shoulder with the screener. As the player approaches the screen, small steps to slow down around the screen create a tight space so the defender can't

get through. Players' hands should be ready, and players should step into the pass. Players should not wait for a pass but rather go forward and receive the ball.

Shooters who spot up should wait for the ball to be thrown directly at target hands. Spotting-up shots often come when the defense plays zone; they are not shot as fast as those that come off screens, but they are still shot fast.

Small Steps

- Small steps are required at times when shooting the ball.

- The term "air step" refers to the action of a player catching the ball and barely taking a step. This step is good to use to quickly get the shot off.

- Small steps are important when trying to slow down. At some point players have to learn to shoot in a controlled manner. Taking small steps will allow players to control themselves better.

Pivot Foot

- Stepping into a shot with correct footing varies depending on the player and coach.

- Some coaches believe in stepping with the same foot, always having a permanent pivot foot. This might be fine for younger players, but the more

advanced players should be taught to switch.

- The quickest and most effective way to step into a shot is with a switching pivot foot, meaning stepping with the foot closest to the basket when turning to square up and shoot.

67

FOUL SHOTS
The same routine must be followed each time

Foul shooting requires a great deal of concentration and routine. The foul line is a place for players to get a quick breather, gather their thoughts, and, if need be, quickly talk to teammates and coaches. Coaches must take this opportunity to let their players know of any new strategies for the game.

If the opposing team shoots a foul shot, make sure players are placed in the proper position in the lane area to be able to box out and get the rebound. The tallest players and best rebounder should be in the square above the box. Players then line up side by side to box out each other. Players cannot go into the paint until the ball touches the rim. Make sure a player boxes out the person shooting the foul shot. If an air ball is shot, or if the ball doesn't hit the rim, the whistle will be blown, and the foul shooter will get another shot, depending on how many shots he was awarded. Or the other team will get the ball from out of bounds.

Stance

- After receiving the ball from the referee, players need to center themselves in the middle of the foul line.

- The right or left foot should not be in the center. Doing so will result in the player shifting to the left. Instead, the basket should fall between both legs.

- This allows the ball to be straight and centered.

- Feet are shoulder width apart and even, and knees must be bent.

- With knees bent, in one motion the player pushes up to release the ball.

Routine

- A routine is the most important thing to do before shooting a foul shot.

- Developing a routine and sticking with it will allow players to relax.

- After the feet are set, the routine should be performed. Players can dribble a few times, spin the ball, or fix shots. Whatever the routine is, it should be done every time the player goes to the foul line.

- Players can fix the ball so that the seams go left to right. Remember that players have only ten seconds to shoot.

If a player jumps over the foul line when shooting a foul shot, the basket will not count. However, younger players are allowed to jump over the foul line in league play. The question of whether a player should jump when shooting a foul shot is often asked. The answer is simple: It depends on the player. If a player has a hard time reaching the basket, a small jump will allow him to reach it better. Taking a small step back will prevent players from jumping over the line. As players get stronger, they do not have to jump, but this usually doesn't happen until high school.

Ready to Shoot

- After players receive the ball from the referee, their feet and body should be set in the proper stance. Next they should follow their routine.

- Players must look at the basket and should wait about two seconds to shoot the foul shot.

- Fouls shots are shot in a slow, controlled manner. There is no rush.

- At the same time, shooting players do not want to take too long. This can cause the players getting ready to box out to go over the lane line.

Release

- The foul shot release is the same as that of the jump shot, except there is no high jumping.

- Youth players may jump to reach a basket or take a small step back to prevent going over the line.

- The youngest players are allowed to jump over the line. If a player does not jump, the player must end on his tiptoes. This allows for more strength and prevents the ball from being pushed.

- Follow-through is the same on all shots.

THREE-POINT SHOTS

Don't dwell on these shots with young players

Three-point shots are shot from behind the arc. The most important thing for players to remember when shooting these shots is that the body's form does not change. If players change their form, they are shooting too far away. Shooting comes from using leg strength, not from pushing or throwing the ball to try to reach the basket.

Three-point shots should be practiced minimally in youth basketball. The three-point line can make younger players develop poor shooting habits that you'll have to correct later. Spending a lot of time on three-point shots is a waste for young players. This skill set should be introduced into practices only after players develop strength and consistently shoot the correct way.

Many players think they need to shoot differently when they are behind the line. This is a bad habit to break. When players shoot around before practice, they should shoot with

Advantages of Three-point Shots

- A team can catch up in a hurry.

- A team can open up the defense.

- Players can have fun with other players and fans.

- Players can create driving opportunities.

- A team can change how the opposing team defends.

Three-point Shots

- Three-point shots are shot the same way as a jump shot but with more emphasis on leg strength. The farther back a player shoots from, the more strength is needed.

- The form never changes when shooting a three-pointer except when the player is out of range.

- If a player is fouled shooting a three-point shot and misses, he shoots three foul shots.

- If a player is fouled shooting a three-point shot and makes the basket, the player is awarded one foul shot for a possible four-point play.

close, game-like shots. Players need to be taught to start in close and work their way out.

Players should understand that they are allowed to jump over the three-point line after they shoot the ball. They must, however, be behind the line before they shoot. If a foot is on the line before the shot is started, the basket will only count for two points.

Teaching Three-point Shots

- When teaching and practicing three-point shots, have the team gradually move back. Start three-point drills at the foul line extended and then take a step back. Move again and have players stand on the three-point line. Finally move again behind line. Many players have mental blocks and change

  shot because they see this three-point line. By teaching this way it gradually gets players to move behind the line and shoot correctly.

- Let players start to shoot three-pointers around twelve years of age. Starting too early will result in poor shooting habits.

Watch the Line

- The three-point line extends around the key and is 19 feet 9 inches from the basket. There is also a line behind it on some courts. This line is for college play.

- Recreational courts as well as public parks have the same distance as high school courts.

- A basket will not count for three points if a player's foot is on the line when releasing the ball. Both feet must be behind the line. Players are allowed to jump over the line after the ball is released.

- If the shot is made, both of the ref's hands go up into the air.

71

TECHNIQUE
Every ounce of bounce should have a purpose

Dribbling allows a team to move the ball up the court without passing. Every dribble should have a purpose. The dribble, pass, and shot are the triple threat of basketball that every player must have. Fundamental ball-handling skills must be practiced on a consistent basis.

Fundamentals of dribbling are as follows: Use the fingertips and pads of the fingers, never the palm. Younger players will tend to slap at the ball. They should push the ball hard off the ground, allowing it to come up in a controlled manner. The ball should never come above the waist. Many times the ball will be dribbled around the knee area. Dribbling takes place slightly off to the side of the body for protection from the defender. Although the player can sometimes bounce the ball across in front of the body, he should not keep it there. Doing so gives the defender a chance to steal the ball. Finally, when dribbling, players should look up, not at the ground or at the ball.

Beginner Dribbling

- Younger players beginning to dribble should concentrate on staying low and keeping head up, dribbling with right and left hand.

- At this age, players tend to dribble around with no direction. Teach players to use both hands and look up to find teammates.

- Teach the hand that isn't dribbling to be used as an arm guard to protect the ball.

- Set up an obstacle course with cones so players can work on changing direction and keep their head up to see where they are going.

Middle Age Player Dribbling

- At this age, players should work on different moves.

- Players need to work on crossover dribble and hesitation dribble. The crossover dribble is to pass the ball from one hand to the next trying to go past the defender. Hesitation dribble is a dribble that, when going full speed, has the player slow up and then burst by a player.

- Remind players not to pick up dribble until they know where they are going with the ball.

When a player switches the ball from one hand to the other, the ball should be bounced in a hard, quick manner. When a player switches directions, he should switch his body toward the direction he is going. A player should always dribble the ball with the outside hand, especially when going at an angle. When dribbling against a defender, a player should always protect the ball with his body and opposite hand.

Advanced Player Dribbling

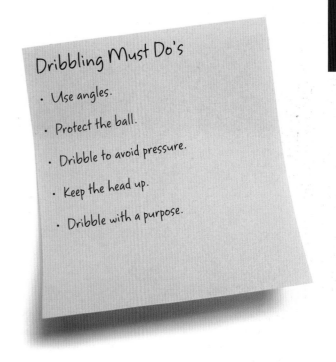

Dribbling Must Do's

- Use angles.
- Protect the ball.
- Dribble to avoid pressure.
- Keep the head up.
- Dribble with a purpose.

- Advanced players should dribble with a purpose and be taught to dribble in a north/south direction with small movements to the side.

- Players should learn the behind-the-back dribble, behind the legs, and the use of double moves.

- Double moves are moves that are used right after one another. For example, doing a behind the back dribble then a crossover is considered a double move.

- Players need to be creative with their dribble, but not too fancy.

73

DIFFERENT MOVES
Players can attack weaknesses of the defense

After players have mastered the basic dribble technique, it's time to move on to actual moves. Dribble moves allow offensive players to attack defensive players and make a move toward their weakness. One of the most important ways to go by a defender is to use angles and to keep the defender off balance. Keeping the head up allows players to see where they are going and to be able to pass to their teammates.

Several moves are used in basketball. Most popular is the crossover and shake move. This move is also known as the "hesitation dribble." The speed dribble is used by all ages but very much so by younger players. The speed dribble is used to quickly advance the ball up the floor. The speed dribble can be done by pushing the ball in front and then catching up to it. After the defense puts on pressure, a control dribble is required. This dribble should be lower around the knee area.

Crossover Dribble

- The crossover dribble is simply a low bounce below the knees, pushing the ball from one hand to the other.

- The crossover dribble can be used to go by a defender or simply to change hands.

- Crossovers are done in front of the body. Players must be careful not to cross over in a lazy fashion because the ball can be stolen.

- The opposite hand should be ready to receive the ball. This allows for a quick crossover. The player should shift weight past the defender by pushing forward.

Hesitation or Shake Dribble

- This is one of the more popular moves, also called the "shake and bake."

- It combines a head and shoulder fake and "stutter" steps, which are short, quick, parallel steps.

- With the ball slightly off to the side and in a low body position, the player dribbles with the right hand, fakes to the left with the left foot, and quickly cuts the shoulder back to the right, moving past the defender.

- This is also a hesitation move because players slow up to do stutter steps, then explode by the defense.

Dribbling to avoid pressure allows players to stay away from traps and to avoid getting caught in corners. They can avoid running up the sidelines and picking the ball up after crossing half court. Players should dribble up the middle of the court while changing directions.

GREEN ● LIGHT

Teach players to use an "exit dribble" to avoid corners or traps. Players should never pick up the ball; instead they should continue dribbling in a sliding backward manner. The "exit dribble" will get players out of trouble situations. Players must use a combination of different moves to beat defenders.

Between-the-legs Dribble

- This dribble is a quick way to move the ball from one hand to the other when a player is closely guarded.

- Players should keep the dribble low. They should put the right hand on the outside part of the ball and push hard between the separated legs.

- Right-handed players tend to start the ball in the right hand and step with the left foot to put the ball through.

- The left hand is ready to receive the ball close to the legs with fingers pointing down to the ground.

Behind-the-back Dribble

- The player should cut as close to the defender as possible. The player should not look back at the ball. The ball should come around back without the player having to turn her head.

- The palm is placed on the outside of the ball to cup the ball over the back area, pushing the ball to the left side and hand. Player should extend arm as close as possible to opposite hip.

- Players should practice doing behind-the-back dribbles with only the dominent hand. This forces players to really push the ball around the back.

STATIONARY DRIBBLING DRILLS

These drills develop confidence for young players on the court who are first learning their skills

Stationary dribbling should be the first thing taught when a player learns to dribble. Stationary dribbling is done standing in one place in a controlled manner. This type of dribbling allows players to develop a feel for the basketball and develop quick hands. The more hours spent dribbling the ball the better players will become.

This is one of the only skills in basketball that doesn't require a large space. Dribbling can be practiced anywhere. Dribbling skills will only develop through hard work and repetition. Players learning to dribble should focus on an object on the wall and stare at the object to avoid looking at the ball. Blinder goggles can also be used to prevent players from

Quickhands

- Developing hand strength at a young age is critical in handling the basketball.

- Getting younger players familiar with the grip of the ball allows dribbling to become easy.

- Players develop quick hands by doing drills to improve this area.

- Drills such as tapping the ball back and forth using only finger tips while moving it up and down the body are good.

- Slapping the ball will get a player's hands warmed up and establish a good grip.

Stationary Crossover

- Stationary crossover can be done at three different levels: Low, medium, and high.

- Low crossover is done below knees. Feet are shoulder width apart. The ball is passed quickly from one hand to the other while the opposite hand waits with the fingers in a downward motion to receive the ball.

- Medium crossover is done in same manner as low crossover but at waist level.

- High crossover is hard to control. This dribble is done for drill purposes only controlling ball crossing over at chest level.

looking at the ball. Another way to improve dribbling is to wear gloves. Winter gloves will cause the ball to slip off of the glove, making it hard to handle. Dribbling a tennis ball is also a very good way to develop hand-eye coordination.

Stationary dribbling can be done without actually dribbling the ball. Drills such as wrapping the ball around the waist, knees, and head will develop quick hands. Stationary dribbling can be done while sitting on the ground. Players can dribble to the side of their bodies. They can also do sit-ups and dribble the ball. They can dribble under their legs by

lifting the legs up together and dribbling the ball under to the other side.

Players should focus on keeping their eyes on one of the nets in the gym when doing stationary drills to improve dribbling because that is where a player's vision should be in a game. Start stationary drills slow and then pick up speed until the ball is fumbled so that players will know their limits.

Dribble Around the Leg

- Dribbling around legs helps develop quick hands and finger tip control of the ball.

- Stand shoulder width apart. Place the ball in the right hand. Start dribbling in a low manner around the back part of the knee. As the ball approaches the back of the sneaker, cup it so the

ball goes back around the right leg. The dribble is then dribbled with the same hand and repeated.

- Switching to the left leg allows players to work on weak hands. Add a figure 8 sequence to it. Remember, dribbles are small with only the use of the fingertips.

In-and-Out Dribble

- The "in-and-out" dribble is very similar to the crossover; however, the ball stays in the same hand.

- Do not carry the ball when doing this drill; the hand must stay on top of it, not under and over.

- Practice this dribble by dribbling midway between the legs and bring the ball back to the start in an "in-and-out" motion. The ball stays in front of the body.

- This drill can also be practiced on the side of the body, called "side slam."

FULL-COURT DRIBBLING DRILLS

If the dribble can't help, pass to teammates

Full court dribbling obviously moves the ball up the court on offense. Whether a player uses a speed or control dribble, the ball must get up the court. Once in the open court, the ball needs to be pushed as fast as the player can go, but in a controlled manner. Limit dribbles in the open court by pushing the ball from one hand to the other. Dribbling just with one hand will result in too many dribbles. Advanced players can dribble the ball from baseline to baseline in about five dribbles.

Full court dribble lines should be an essential part of practice. Use a variation of dribbles that will be performed in games. Jump stopping on the baseline and working on use of the pivot foot is a good way to turn back around and continue dribble moves. Younger players should work on two or three moves. Do not introduce behind back or between legs.

These dribble moves are too difficult for younger players. The more advanced players can incorporate dribble moves

Dribble Lines

- Dribble lines are ideal for beginner players. Start simple by having them dribble stationary; blow the whistle to indicate the start.

- Lines of three players each will allow many turns. Change dribbles from right to left hand and from control to speed dribble.

- Keep it basic and reinforce the proper dribble form.

- Teach crossover dribble; make sure players run, not hop, when doing crossover and that the ball is in the hand of the direction they're in.

Dribble Lines with Moves

- Dribble lines can be used to make moves at certain points on the court.

- Using the foul line, half court, and opposite foul line allows players to make moves in those three areas.

- Using a variation of dribble moves allows players to mix and match.

- Double moves are also ideal to help players by defenders. For example, try a shake move into a crossover.

into shooting drills. These drills should be done full court so players can work on three aspects of dribbling: 1) Pushing the ball up court, 2) Making a move, and 3) Dribbling in a controlled manner. Slowing down before shooting allows players to step into shots in a controlled manner.

Big Step Dribble

- Take a big step to get past the defense.

- When a player is in a triple threat position, the first step should be a big step with the ball being pushed low and in front of the lead foot.

- The player must stretch her body out and get as close to the defender as possible. Dribble in a north/south direction, not east/west.

- Protect the ball with the body, with momentum moving forward to take up space.

Limited Dribbles

- Limited dribbles are for advanced players. Limiting dribbles allows the player to get up court quicker.

- Do not dribble the ball with the same hand; switching hands pushes the ball up court faster.

- Advanced players should be able to make a layup starting at the three point line with one dribble.

- When dribbling, don't take too many dribbles to get to a spot on the floor. Take big strides and dribble with a purpose.

TWO BALL DRIBBLING DRILLS
Dribble stationary first with two balls, and then start moving

Two ball dribbling dramatically increases a player's dribbling and ball handling skills. Dribbling two basketballs at a time is a lot harder to do than one ball. It requires the player to concentrate more.

Start dribbling two balls without moving. Two balls are difficult to do for younger players. Do not waste time in practice doing this. A problem arises sometimes when doing two ball drills. Players complain one ball doesn't bounce as high as the other ball. To fix this problem, simply have the ball that bounces higher placed in the player's weaker hand. This allows the player to control both balls better.

Two ball drills should be practiced many times stationary before moving up the court. Once the stationary two balls are mastered, slowly progress into moving up court. At first, balls will knock into each other and kids will chase them all over the court.

Two Balls Stationary

- Two balls stationary dribbling should be done with both balls having equal amount of air. If one ball is low on air, this will have an effect on the drill.

- Both need to be dribbled in a controlled manner. If one ball is dribbled in a soft manner, this will have an effect on the drill.

- Dribble both balls evenly low, medium, and then high.

- Alternate the dribbles in a one-two, one-two fashion and with altering speeds (low, medium, and high).

Two Balls In/Out

- Two balls in and out drill can be done two ways.

- The first way is to dribble both balls evenly in front of the body and then move each ball in an "in-and-out" fashion. Be weary of balls hitting each other.

- The second way is to dribble both balls evenly in front of the body, then have them go in the same direction. The balls are still dribbled in the "in-and-out" manner but in the same direction.

Start by having kids dribble stationary on the baseline so they can get control of the balls and then slowly walk up the court. As progression takes place have them start a light jog and then eventually get to a faster dribble. With this drill, players develop the use of their weaker hands.

Two Balls Full Court

- Two balls dribbling full court is same as stationary dribbling but adds movement up the court.

- This forces the player to get into proper dribbling form.

- Start players dribbling in a stationary manner; blow the whistle for them to start up the court. Both balls should be dribbled evenly. Eventually add a light jog and then a run.

- Balls can also be dribbled in an alternate manner.

Two Balls Zigzag

- This drill should be done with advanced players only.

- Start players dribbling stationary; blow the whistle to indicate moving up the court. Players dribble the ball evenly moving to the right, taking about three steps and dribbles. Players then move their body to the left and take three steps left. The process is repeated in a zigzag fashion up the court.

- This drill can be done with the alternate dribble as well.

81

CHAIR DRIBBLING

A chair acts as a defensive player as well as a person setting a screen

There are many training devices used to help players become better skilled, from blinders to weighted basketballs. It's all out there for players to buy. The most popular and useful training device is the simple chair. A chair can be found in any gym and can be used for many purposes. The chair can be used as a defender, a person setting a screen, or to help players shoot behind something. Younger players have a tendency to jump forward and throw their bodies to their shots. By having a chair in front of them, this prevents the player from jumping forward.

The chair is very useful in allowing players to make a move behind the chair. Players dribble up to the chair, make a move

Dribble Move at Chair

- A chair will act as a defender. By doing dribble moves at a chair, players understand that a person will be in front of them and they must move slightly to the side and forward to go by.

- Use various moves at the chair during practice drills. Players can make a move and go in for a layup or jump shot.

- Several chairs can be used as well.

Dribbling Around Chair

- Dribbling around a chair will simulate dribbling off of a screen.

- Dribbling around a chair helps younger players with proper footwork. It forces them to step into the shot with the correct foot.

- Working on both the left and right side helps players understand using the inside pivot foot.

- Remind players to get as close as possible to the chair, stimulating coming off of a screen.

and then drive to basket. Players also can dribble off of the chair, simulating dribbling off a screen. Chairs also hold basketballs in place. Placing a ball in the seat of the chair allows the player to pick up the ball in a low stance and shoot the ball or dribble right or left. Sitting in a chair can be a useful teaching device. Players sit on the edge of the chair and dribble out of it. Players cannot stand up; they must stay low and dribble low to the area to shoot.

ZOOM

When making a move, players should visualize dribbling under a shelf. This will force them to stay low. A second visual is to pretend they are in a refrigerator box and can't make a move outside of the box. They have to stay within the box.

Shooting Behind Chair

- Dribbling up to the chair allows younger players to not throw their body into shot.

- Dribbling up to the chair also provides an object in front of the player, simulating someone playing defense.

- Using the width of a standard chair helps shooters align their feet properly with the chair.

- Players will learn not to jump forward after awhile; if they do, they will end up hitting the chair.

Sitting in Chair

- This drill allows players to work on staying low when dribbling the basketball.

- Start by sitting on the edge of the chair. Have one leg forward, the other leg on the side of the chair.

- Start dribbling ball; after about three stationary dribbles, slightly rise up from the chair and move forward, dribbling in a low fashion. Take about three more dribbles forward into the shot.

- Do not stand up from the chair. This will defeat the purpose of drill.

TECHNIQUES

A team can move the ball up the court quickly

The quickest way to get the basketball up the court is by passing. Several different passes are used throughout the game. The two most common passes are the chest pass and the bounce pass. These two passes are similar in nature; however, one is thrown through the air, whereas the other is bounced between players.

When throwing the ball, players must step forward toward the person receiving the ball to put more power behind the pass. Certain passes require a different foot to step first. Passing requires players to be in an athletic stance to be able to move around the defender. The pivot foot is important in passing because it allows the player to move around without walking to see the open person. Regardless of the pass type, a push forward with a thrust of both arms and a snap of the wrist ensures that the ball gets to the target person. Extending the arms in a follow-through manner also adds power.

Proper Passing Form

- Making passes to set up shots and execute offense requires proper passing form.

- Stepping to the passer is critical, but players should not overextend the step. This tends to take away some balance.

- Players should extend arms and palms outward for a basic chest pass. A backspin off the ball will be seen because the position of the thumbs goes from up to down. The backspin makes the ball easier to catch.

- Extending the arms increases the strength of a pass.

Target Hands

- Here hands are open with fingers in an upward placement. Hands should be in the shape of a "W" with thumbs almost touching each other.

- Players should get open as much as possible to present a good target for passers.

- Remember that a good pass is good only if it is caught.

- Not every pass is perfect; players should always be ready to move if a pass is not good or to regain balance before throwing another pass.

The player receiving the ball should have hands ready around her chest area. Hand position should be in the shape of a "W," hands open with fingers wide and thumbs almost touching each other. A player should never catch a ball with the chest but rather catch a ball slightly away from the chest. Advanced players will learn to position their hands to shoot the ball immediately.

Here are several key points to remember when teaching: Passes should be crisp and reach targets with force; no floating passes. Eye contact should be made between the two players. Balls should never be thrown too low or behind or over a player's head. Players become better passers by getting the ball to the right player at the right time.

Ready Passing Position

- When passing a ball, players should never stand up. A bent position or athletic stand ensures that the pass gets to the receiver.

- Younger players tend to stand with feet close together and throw from the forehead. This habit must be corrected. Passes must be thrown from waist level with the exception of the overhead pass.

- Players must always step when passing—no exceptions.

- Players use unspoken signals to pass the ball. Passers must be aware of this.

Jumping to Ball

- Stepping forward or "jumping to ball" with ready hands prevents the defense from jumping in front and stealing the ball.

- A player should keep her eyes on the ball from the time it leaves the passer's hands until the ball touches the receiver's hands.

- Upon catching, the player should bend her elbows slightly and bring the ball toward her chest. This cushions the impact of the pass and gives better control. It also puts shooters in a ready position.

DIFFERENT WAYS OF PASSING
Teach the fundamentals to set up good shots

The more passes made by the offense, the more the defense starts to scramble. The defense then becomes tired and frustrated. Passes by the offense must be quick and effective. The result of well-executed passes is a shot on the opponent's basket.

A chest pass is thrown when there isn't a defense player between the two offensive players. The ball is held with both hands chest high and passed to the target. A bounce pass is similar to a chest pass; however, the ball is bounced before it reaches the target. Bounce passes are used during fast breaks, leading players who cut to the basket for a layup. Bounce passes are also used for players cutting to the backdoor or for post players calling for the ball. A bounce pass is also effective when a player is being closely guarded.

The two-handed overhead pass is used several times during a game. It can be used as an outlet pass when a player

Chest Pass

- The chest pass can be practiced anytime. This is the first pass that players will learn.

- Make sure younger players don't pull the ball too close into their chest and that they don't use their body to throw the ball. Instead, they should throw the ball slightly away from the chest.

- Chest passes can be used in several shooting drills.

- A chest pass is a great way to start an offense. Proper passing angles are essential in executing the offense.

Bounce Pass

- The bounce pass should travel from the player's waist to the receiver's waist.

- The ball should bounce at about halfway to the receiver.

- Follow-through should be the same as for the chest pass. Bending the legs puts strength behind the pass.

- The backspin slows the ball when it hits the ground so it's easier to catch.

gets the rebound to pass to a guard. It can be used to pass the ball around the perimeter and can be used as a "skip pass" over the defense.

Players must be able to see where the defense is when passing. Players should attack the defense's weak areas and pass away from the defensive players. Great passers have great peripheral vision. With peripheral vision a player can see teammates off to the side without turning the head. Good passers should know the proper pass to execute. By reading the defensive players, they can make proper passes. A good rule of thumb is to pass around or under a taller opponent and over a shorter one. Players should never hold a ball behind the head and should always move the ball around along with the pivot foot to find an open player.

Overhead Pass

- This pass has several purposes: As a pass around perimeter, as a skip pass, and, most importantly, as an outlet pass.

- When a player gets a rebound, she must keep the ball overhead out of reach of opposing players. From this position an over-the-head pass is thrown to the guard.

- The ball is thrown in a forceful manner, staying above the head; a player should not drop the ball below the head.

- The overhead pass should be a direct hard pass to target, not a lob.

Hook Pass

- A hook pass is an accurate pass into post. The hook pass requires the player to step with either foot around the defense.

- The hand is cupped around the ball. The wrist is then flicked and pushed toward the receiver.

- Advanced players will be able to add a slight spin to make the ball turn in the direction in which they throw.

- Players need to read the court—know where the defense is playing—to pass into a post.

DRILLS: 6–9-YEAR-OLDS
Teach younger players three basics

When teaching younger players to pass, give them three passes to master: Chest pass, bounce pass, and overhead pass. These are the three most used passes in the game.

It's important to get your players used to calling out each others names so their teammates are aware the ball is coming to them. Calling names helps players get to know each other and work as a team as well as lets them to know that a pass is coming.

Teach younger players to always have target hands ready around the chest area to prevent injury. A good way to remind younger players of the proper position of target hands is to have them make a "W" shape with their hands, that is, hands open with both thumbs touching each other. Younger players also tend to throw bad passes when receiving a bad pass from another player. Teach players to regain balance before making a pass.

Line Passing

- This is the most basic drill to learn how to pass. This drill should be done with beginner players.

- Have players partner up according to ability or height.

- Players will partner up standing about 8 feet across from one another. Partners will work on different passes and catching the ball. If players have a hard time reaching each other, move them closer.

- Coaches should change pass types after two or three minutes of practicing a particular type of pass.

Circle Passing

- Circle passing is a good way for players to learn teammates' names and to focus on catching the ball.

- All players circle around one player in the middle. The middle player passes the ball to another player, who then passes back to the middle person. The middle person then passes to the next person in the circle, who also passes back to the middle. This continues until every player gets a pass. After that happens, a new player goes to the middle.

- Names of the pass receivers must be called with each pass.

Teaching players to receive the ball also requires them to step to pass. Many times these players wait for the ball instead of meeting the ball. The opposite also happens from the passing end. There are times when players do not take a step toward their target. This causes the ball to be passed more slowly and stolen by the defense.

Make sure that a hard, forceful pass is not performed by two players close to each other. This should be demonstrated to players in practice to avoid injury. Younger players need to learn to hold on to the ball and to squeeze the ball when it is caught. Players should never lose eye contact with the ball; when they do, they will not catch the ball. They will fumble, which will result in a walk.

Monkey in the Middle

- This drill focuses on passing under pressure. Players are in several groups of three on court: Two offensive players and one defensive.

- One offensive player starts with the ball. The defensive player applies pressure on the ball, trying to steal it or to get a hand on it.

- One offensive player pivots around the defense, trying to pass to the other offensive player. Any pass is allowed.

- If the defense touches or steals the ball from a player, the two players switch roles.

Wall Passing

- Wall passing helps develop quick hands and reactions and improves chest and bounce passes. It is done when a player passes the ball to a wall and the ball comes back to the player to catch.

- Wall passing improves reflexes and form and doesn't require another person. Remember that arm strength will be developed over time.

- Coaches should be aware that younger players will get tired and that their arms will hurt. Do these drills in small sets. They will get a lot of passes in because the ball comes back quickly.

DRILLS: 10–12-YEAR-OLDS
Teach players different types of passes to use in different situations

At the middle-aged level, players have mastered the three basic passes. Different passes should now be taught. Players should realize that they are passing for a purpose. Finding the open player for a shot and executing the offense are important at this level. Emphasis should be on keeping the head up to find open players, starting to develop entry passes, and feeding the ball into post.

As players' skills get better, more players develop easier and faster ways to pass. The hook pass is a useful pass to use when passing into post. This pass is done by passing around the defense by hooking the leg around and hooking the arm to bounce the ball to the player posting up.

The baseball pass is another pass used to advance the ball up court. This long-distance pass is thrown more than half the court and is useful in getting a quick basket when players run ahead on a fast break or when a player is alone.

Slide Passing

- This drill is similar to line passing.

- Players start on the baseline. Players should be partnered up again by ability or height. In this drill players slide up court while passing the ball to a partner.

- Players should slide even with each other. Passes should be made to the chest area. Remind players not to pass behind their partner.

- Players change passes as the drill continues. Remember that target hands should always be up and ready to catch a pass.

Multiple Ball Passing

- Players form groups of five and form a medium-size circle.

- Here the ball starts with one player who passes to a designated person. This person then passes to another person and so forth until the passes form a star pattern, so everyone throws the ball to the same person. Players stay in circle and do not move.

- After players master one ball, throw in a second. Players must continue to pass to the same person. Different passes must be used because balls will hit each other. Add up to five balls.

The push pass and off-the-dribble pass have gained popularity over the years. A push pass starts around the shoulder area; hand position is the same as when shooting the ball. When the pass is made, it can be straight or a lob. Push passes are controlled, accurate passes. The off-the-dribble pass is done in a quick, deceptive manner and is useful in passing during a fast break. To make the pass work, the hand should move slightly to the side of the ball on the last dribble. The ball is pushed in a forceful manner to a receiver.

Dribble passing, like shooting, requires repetition. However, the only way for a team to be an effective passing team, to know when to pass and which pass to throw, is to play against defensive pressure.

Jump Stop Passing

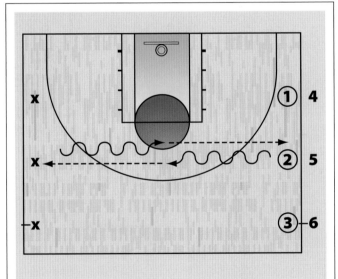

- Here, player 2 dribbles to the middle, jump stops, and passes to the X, who is in front of her.

- Player 2 follows the pass and becomes the next player in line.

- The X will then dribble to the middle, jump stop, and pass to player 5.

- She will then follow her pass to the end of the line.

Star Passing

- This drill can also be done by adding a shot to it. This drill starts with six players situated in a star pattern—two players at opposite wings, two players in opposite corners, and one player in front of the basket. Another player waits behind the player under the basket.

- Players pass to the same spot, forming a star pattern. After a pass is made, the player then follows the pass and replaces the player who left the spot. This continues.

- Change passes and be sure that names are called before passing.

DRILLS: 13–14-YEAR-OLDS
Transition drills develop skills in older players

Advanced players will face a lot of defensive pressure in games. Players must understand by now which pass to throw. Passing the ball immediately is sometimes not an option. In many cases a fake is used to get the defender to move. Players must understand the different lanes they can pass through. The lanes vary depending on what a player's defensive stance is or whether he is jumping. The majority of the time the lanes that are open are over the top of the defender's head, the right or left side of the head, and the right or left side of the defender's leg.

When running a fast break, players without the ball must run wide out into passing lanes while running down court. This makes it hard on the defense to play all players. The wider players run, the harder it is for the defense. After the offensive players cross the foul line plane, then they must run in toward the basket to receive the ball for a layup.

Passing into Shot

- Two lines are formed on the baseline. One line has basketballs; the other is lined up even with the three-point line to the right, but on the baseline.

- One player (A) with a ball passes back and forth to a partner (B) while running. As the players approach the foul line plane, player A dribbles the ball a few times to get to the foul line and jump stop, while player B cuts to the basket and receives pass for a layup.

- This is a great drill for passing accuracy and timing.

Lead Pass

- A lead pass is thrown during a fast break.

- This pass is thrown by a player to her teammate by passing ahead. The player pushes her arms up and releases the ball.

- This motion provides a higher, softer pass that lands on the court and bounces up to the teammate to grab in stride.

- The receiver should secure the ball with both hands and proceed with a fast break.

The player with the ball must push it up court and find the open player ahead. This player should be in the middle of the court so he has the option of passing to the left or right side. The player should always pass a ball ahead, never behind, to an open player. This is called a "lead pass." The player passing should stop at the foul line, giving enough space to pass a ball. At this point a bounce pass or off-the-dribble pass should be performed. Many drills work on getting passes up the court, including two-on-zero passing, three-man weave, two-on-one fast break, and pass outlet drill. These drills can use different passes and incorporate both offensive and defensive transitions into the lesson.

Full-court Team Passing

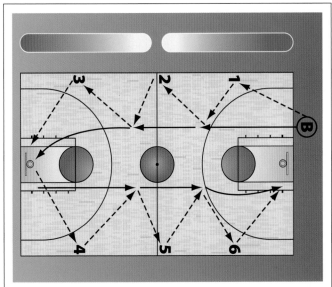

- Here, player B passes on the outside while the other players start on the baseline with basketballs.

- The ball is passed to the first passer, who passes the ball back. The ball is then thrown to the second passer and back. And, finally, the ball is passed to the third passer, and back in for a shot.

- This continues on the outside, as well. Players end up passing to all six passers.

- Continue for three minutes and then switch positions.

Passing Drill into Layup

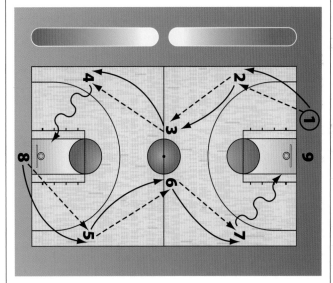

- This is a great conditioning and passing drill. Players are in six spots. The remaining players line up under the basket, where they pass the ball to the wing player. Players should follow their passes.

- The next player passes to the middle player. The third basket player passes to the wing player, who dribbles in for a layup.

- This continues on the other side.

93

GUARDS

Being able to play all positions makes players valuable on the court

Despite the changes to the game over the years, fundamentals have remained pretty much the same. Players now are more versatile and are able to play many positions. The guards on the basketball court consist of the point guard and off guard.

The point guard position requires the player to run the offense and be a leader on the court. This player must possess many important qualities. He must be a good ball handler and passer, have an instinctive knowledge of the game, be able to penetrate and pass to teammates, be a good dribbler with both hands, and be able to hit an outside shot when left open.

The off guard, also known as the "shooting guard" or "number 2 guard," is generally the best shooter on the court. This player must be able to hit shots consistently from 15 to 20 feet away, must be able to move without the ball to get

Point Guard

- Point guards tend to be shorter. These players are quick, with excellent dribbling skills.

- The point spot on the court is at the top of the key, stretching back to the center circle.

- Point guards should lead the team in assists and steals. They must play hard-nosed defense and be able to stop dribble penetration.

- Point guards should also know basketball lingo.

Shooting Guard

- This guard has duties similar to those of the point guard but usually doesn't bring the ball up court.

- This position usually takes the most shots in the game. Many screens can be set for the guards to get open for a shot.

- A player who can combine the skills of both a point guard and shooting guard can be dangerous on the court.

open, must be able to drive to the basket, must be able to shoot three-point shots, and must have an instinctive knowledge of the game.

The point guard usually announces specific plays and basically starts the plays. He acts like a coach on the court, similar to a quarterback in football. A point guard sets the tone and speed of play for the team. The point guard sets the tempo of the game by pushing the ball up court quickly when opportunity presents itself or brings the ball up in a steady controlled manner to set up a play.

The two guard positions can be interchangeable. Both positions typically encourage other players to do better and celebrate successful plays. Guards must play good pressure defense and must be the first players back when possession is changed to protect their baskets.

Driving to Basket

- Players should limit their dribbles when driving to the basket.

- Players must go full speed when driving to the hoop but in a controlled manner.

- Advanced players should be able to start at the three-point line and take one dribble to the basket to complete the layup.

- When a player shoots a layup after driving to the basket, she should be sure the layup is shot in a controlled, soft-touch manner. Often layups are missed because a player goes too fast or is out of control.

Tips for Guard Play

- Get open: Perimeter players will often need to create space from their defenders.

- Post entry pass: This necessary pass must be mastered by guards. This pass goes down to a player who posts up a defender.

- Know when to run: Know when to fast break and when to slow the ball down.

- Be a triple threat: Guards should be able to shoot, pass, and dribble.

95

FORWARD & CENTER

The inside player should be able to play both facing the basket and facing away from the basket

The forward and center inside positions can also be interchangeable; however, the center position, like the point guard position, tends to stay the same, especially if your team has a dominant center.

The center is typically the tallest player on a team. This player should have strong hands, good strength (both upper and lower body), and good jumping ability. The center must also be able to grab rebounds, both defensively and offensively, and block shots. These players control the paint area. Centers should be able to score from short-range to mid-range areas. This includes being able to do a layup on the right and left sides, being able to post up to receive the ball

Power Forwards

- After the center, the next tallest player is the forward. There are two forwards: Small forward and power forward.

- Forwards can be required to play in the wing and corner areas. Power forwards, however, typically stay in the paint.

- Offensively, power forwards are responsible for getting open, taking outside shots, driving to the basket, and getting rebounds.

- Defensively, power forwards must prevent drives to the basket and get many rebounds.

Small Forwards

- Small forwards pretty much do everything on the basketball court.

- Small forwards should be able to get out on a fast break quickly, drive to the basket, and pull up for a jump shot at any time.

- These players tend to be slightly taller than guards and very athletic. Their body shape is different than that of power forwards in that power forwards tend to be more muscular and battle more inside.

to make a move, and being able to consistently put shots back up after offensive rebounds. Centers must be able to make foul shots. These players will get to the line many times during a game because of the physical contact in the paint.

The small forward and power forward tend to be different. The small forward faces the basket much more and has a finessed look, whereas the power forward is more of an inside player and possesses more power. The small forward is capable of scoring from anywhere, whether it's scoring from the wing, driving to the basket, or scoring in the paint. Small forwards are typically first out on the break and run the court well. These players have good athletic abilities.

The power forward is known for doing the dirty work. This player cleans up the mess of missed shots or sets screens. This player possesses many of the same characteristics of the center, and many of his shots come in the paint. This player is known as the enforcer and is able to stop many opponents from scoring.

Center

- The center is generally positioned near the basket.

- The center position is the last line of defense.

- Offensively, the center's goal is to get open to shoot. He is responsible for setting screens, getting offensive rebounds, and putting the ball back into the basket.

- Centers are expected to get a lot of rebounds because they are taller than most other players.

Court Placement of Players

- High post area: Area that surrounds either end of the foul line where it intersects with the foul lane. Post player position.

- Low post area: Area around block on both sides of lane lines. Post player position.

- Wing: The two shoulders of the court. Guard positions.

- Corner: Formed by sideline and baseline. All positions.

DRILLS FOR GUARDS
Players must practice with intensity and game speed

When incorporating drills into practice, do drills that will enhance players' positions. Do not waste time in practice with drills for skills that players will not use in games.

There are tons of drills for guards. The focus for guards should be on dribbling, shooting, and playing defense. When developing a practice plan, break down drills that will be done offensively, defensively, and then a combination of both. By having all guards working together, they can be competitive but at the same time make each other better.

Coaches shouldn't do the same drills every day. Otherwise, players will get bored and start going through the motions. There are a ton of quality drills out there to be taught. Make use of assistant coaches and managers as passers and rebounders. Have a working clock, if available, to keep track of time. This is typically done in high school practices. Drills should move quickly from one to the next. Players should

Lane Dribbling Drill

- This drill is great for dribbling in boundaries.

- Here two players start at one time. The offensive player (A) starts at the foul line with the ball. Player A dribbles in one place until the whistle is blown.

- Then player A tries to get to the baseline by making moves to get there. The defensive player (B) tries to steal the ball or force the player outside the lane area.

- Player A cannot step outside the lane area. If she does, she loses possession. Player A gets the ball five times before the two switch.

Three-guard Shooting

- Three players are in this drill. One player rebounds, one passes, and another shoots.

- The shooter starts in the corner with the ball. The passer has the other ball. The rebounder should be opposite the shooter.

- Time drill for one minute. The player shoots and slides up to wing area. Ball is passed from passer to shooter again at the wing. Shooter then goes back to the corner to shoot again.

- This rotation of two spots takes place for one minute. Then players rotate.

not walk from one drill to the other. Make sure each drill is done correctly. Having experienced players who understand many drills demonstrate the drills first allows other players to watch and understand what to do. Create a competitive environment by making the losers do push-ups or sprints.

Skip-pass Drill

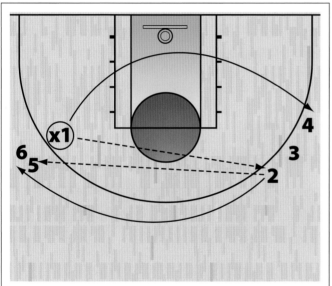

- The skip pass is an over-the-head pass used primarily against zone defenses.

- Here, X1 begins the drill by throwing the ball over the head to player 2, who is standing on the opposite wing.

- X1 cuts along the baseline to the opposite line after making the skip pass.

- Player 2 receives the pass and throws a skip pass to 5. Player 2 then cuts along the top of the key to the opposite line.

L-cut Drill

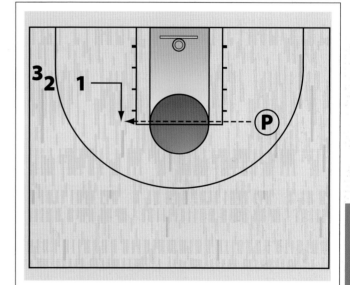

- The L-cut drill is used to teach players how to cut to get open to receive a pass.

- In this drill, player 1 cuts into the lane, planting her baseline foot and quickly

changing direction to go to the elbow.

- This makes an "L" cut.

PLAYER POSITIONS

DRILLS FOR FORWARDS & CENTER

By using their hands, inside players can dictate where they want the ball

As guards do position work, forwards and centers should do the same down at the other end of the court. Again, assistant coaches and managers should be used as passers, especially passing into post. Post players should work on layups, taking quick shots when receiving the ball in post, and rebounding. Many of the drills should be done with defensive pressure to simulate game play. Remember that practice makes perfect.

Drills should be simple and basic in the beginning of the season. Start off by doing layups of all kinds: Power layups, layups on both the right and left sides, and posting up, drop stepping to a layup. After players understand the concept of staying out of the three-second lane and posting up to

Tap Drill at Basket

- This drill emphasizes jumping and keeping the ball above the head.

- Two players stand directly under the basket, side by side. One player will use the right side of the backboard, the other player will use the left side.

- The ball starts over one player's head. She jumps up three times and on the fourth jump shoots the ball.

- Players should repeat this ten times and switch sides. The shot taken is a power layup.

Miken Drill

- This drill is used to work on exploding to the rim when shooting a layup.

- The player starts by facing the basket in front of the rim with the ball about 3 feet away from the rim. She steps with the left foot and shoots off of the glass, doing a right-handed layup.

- She gets the rebound and does the same on the left side, except that she steps with her right foot to do a left-handed layup.

- The ball should never touch the ground. Players shoot about thirty shots each time.

receive the ball, then defensive pressure should be added. Rebounding pads also can be used to make contact with players shooting layups. These pads are used to block players when they go up for shots, simulating player contact.

As players develop their post moves, they can work on shooting short jumpers and facing the basket. Many post drills are taught with backs to the basket. Post players need to learn to do both back-to-basket and facing-basket shots. A good post player will be able to come out of the post and drive to the back or shoot.

Two-ball Power Layup

- This drill is used to get players to quickly put ball into the basket off of the ground and is done for one minute.

- One rebounder, one shooter, and two players place two balls on blocks. Blocks are at the bottom of the key area outside the lane. Players start by picking up one ball from block, shooting a power layup, and then sliding across to pick up the other ball on block. Rebounder passes to the player placing the ball on block. Shooter should always face the basket.

- A baskets equals one point. A good score is over 25.

Rebounding for Younger Players

- This is a good drill to keep younger players from being afraid of the ball and to teach them to jump for the rebound.

- Form one line in front of the basket off to the right side. Throw a ball off of the backboard; the player jumps and grabs the rebound. She turns and throws an outlet pass to a player waiting outside the three-point line in the wing area. The rebounder then replaces the outlet player who received the ball.

TEAM DRILLS FOR ALL POSITIONS

These should be used to get your players to communicate

Now it is time to bring players together after position work. Team drills can be done at anytime during practice. Whether it's a drill in the beginning to warm up the team, a conditioning drill, or a transition drill, players need to get used to playing together. Many team drills incorporate all aspects of the game.

Start by doing fast break conditioning drills. These drills allow players to start moving up and down court. Many

teams are out of shape; you don't want this to happen to yours. Fast break drills promote intensity, concentration, and teamwork, especially if you're trying to get a certain amount of shots in a time period. Start off by doing two-on-zero drills, then three-on-zero, two-on-one, three-on-two, and eventually an eleven-man fast break. Build up from the different transition options until the players are ready for eleven man.

Three-line Shooting

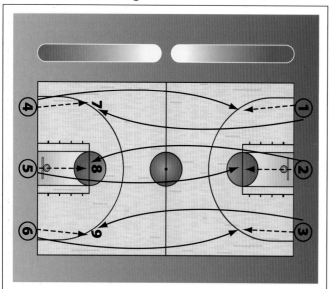

- Three players spread across the baseline with basketballs, and three others spread out across the opposite baseline, also with balls. Finally, three players spread out across the foul line plane.

- The ball is passed to all three shooters on the foul

line, who shoot and get their rebound and then line up on the baseline.

- Players on the baseline sprint down court to the foul line and receive the pass from the baseline passers. They shoot the ball.

Half-court Shooting Drill

- The "1" and "4" start with balls.

- X1 and X2 sprint to the elbow area to receive passes as well as rebound their own shots.

- The "1" and "4" run at the shooters with hands up.

- After passing, the players "1" and "4" continue to the half-court line, turn, and sprint to the elbows to receive passes from "2" and "5."

Full-court shooting drills are great for conditioning and shooting under pressure with the players' hands up. Working up a sweat and simulating game shots allow good habits to form. Players should shoot foul shots in between drills when they are tired. Practicing foul shots when players aren't tired is ineffective. Have players sprint down court when a foul shot is missed.

This drill is done for three minutes. Baskets count as one point. Teams should get at least thirty points.

YELLOW LIGHT

Coaches should be careful to not run too many conditioning drills during midseason. Conditioning should be maintained but not be so intensive as to work players into the ground. Emphasis should be on doing the drill work and running plays. If players are going hard in the drill work, then they will keep themselves in shape.

Continuous Shooting Drill

- The middle line starts with the ball. Two players are down at the opposite end of the court with basketballs on the baseline. Middle player passes to the wing player, gets ball back, and passes to other player moving down court.

- Middle player gets ball back and shoots a layup. Two wing players get the ball from baseline player and shoot from wings. Baseline players now become wings. Middle person grabs any ball and starts drill going at the other end. Middle player shoots layup, and two wings now get passes from opposite baseline players.

Swing Ball Drill

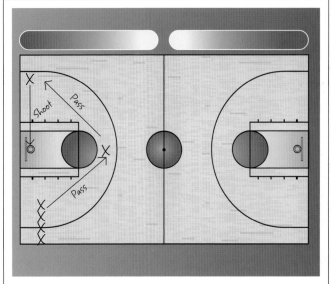

- This is a simple, effective drill that incorporates both shooting and passing.

- Players start in a corner, one player at the top, the other in the corner. The ball is passed to the top player, who then swings to the corner player, who shoots.

- The shooter gets the rebound and goes to the end of the line. Switch sides and add a three-point shot to the drill.

103

RUNNING PLAYS & SETS
Know which basketball plays to call and when

Coaches need to have several set plays that can be used during a game. Whether it's an out-of-bounds play, a zone offense play, or a half-court man offensive play, players need to know how to execute them all. Running plays allows coaches to get their better players looks at the basket to help their team stay in control and organized and to take advantage of the weaknesses of the other team. As coach, you need to understand the right timing and strategy to call

out a specific play. Plays can be called out over and over, especially if they consistently work. Plays will increase scoring opportunities and allow players to be put into positions to be successful.

Called plays should have names that are easy to remember. Some teams use the names of numbers, colors, or college teams. If you coach younger players, make it as simple as possible. Younger players will not remember all the plays.

Jump Ball

Man Offense

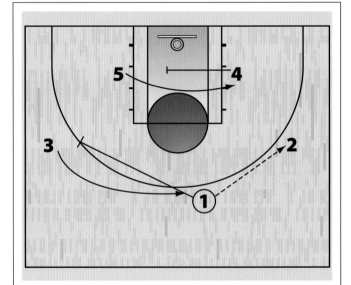

- When games start with a jump ball, players must be in proper position. The tallest player or best jumper will jump ball.

- Always have a defensive player at the foul line behind the teammate jumping.

- Players should match up side by side and be ready for the ball to come to them.

- If your team gets the ball, have a player cut to the basket right away for an easy layup. You may be able to get a quick basket.

- Basic motion offense involves passing, screening, and cutting.

- The above diagram shows the initial movement.

- On the pass from "1" to "2" several things occur: "4" will cross screen for "5," and "1" will screen across for "3."

- The "2" can shoot, pass to "5" on the block, or pass to "3" at the top of the key.

Instead, making sure the players are spaced out and in the right spot will put them into a position to score. Plays can be called out by the coach or point guard. Point guards can also hold up a finger or two indicating which play to run. When the ball is taken out of bounds, the player will slap the ball overhead to indicate that the play should start.

During practice coaches should repeatedly execute plays and make players understand all the options. As coach, you will practice plays that must be run against a defense. Be sure to stop throughout the practice so your players can see what they are doing right or what they are doing wrong. Let the players practice in a controlled scrimmage to allow them to understand better. Incorporating out-of-bounds and pressing situation plays must not be forgotten.

Man and Zone Play

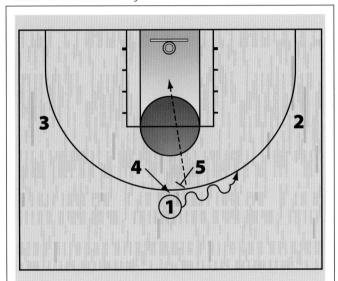

- To start this offense, "1" dribbles off a screen set by "5," who rolls to the middle of the lane, and "4" cuts to the top of the key.

- The "1" can shoot off of the initial screen, pass to "5" rolling or pass to "4," who in turn looks to pass to "5" in the middle of the lane.

- The "5" can shoot or pass to "3" or "2" on the wings.

Zone Play

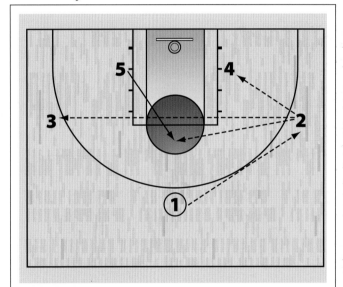

- To start the offense, "1" passes to "2," and several events occur: "4" posts up looking for a pass from "2," and "5" cuts to the middle of the foul line.

- The "2" can shoot, pass to "4" on the block, pass to "5" at the foul line, or skip pass to "3."

VARIOUS CUTS TO GET OPEN
Players must know which one works best

The more open a player is on the court, the more scoring opportunities she will have. Several different cuts can be used. Whether the player comes off a screen or tries to get open by herself, she must create space to get a shot off. In terms of stance, balance is as important as squaring the shoulders and getting the feet set after a cut.

A wide base, shoulder width apart and knees bent, allows players to be ready to shoot, dribble, or pass when receiving the ball. When a player wants to do a quick pivot or change of direction, he should stay on the balls of his feet. This allows the player to move quickly and keep his balance.

Several different cuts can be used throughout the game. The more popular ones are the V cut, L cut, curl cut, and fade cut. The V cut is the easiest cut and the first cut taught to young players. In recent years, the L cut has taken over to get open and is often used when players come off of a screen

L Cut

- The L cut can be used anywhere on the court to get open.

- It is the most popular cut used in the game today.

- When executing the L cut, the offensive player starts by walking a defender up the lane line. When the player is ready, he steps into the defender, making a small amount of contact. Players should not push off. The player should change speed and quickly push off the inside foot to pop out and receive the ball.

V Cut

- V cuts are used often by players on the wings to get open.

- A V cut is a hard fake toward the basket followed by a sharp cut back out toward the ball.

- The key is to sell the cut toward the basket and explode back to the ball. The pattern ends up being shaped into a V formation.

- After players receive the ball they must always square to the basket.

and defense is trailing. Fade cuts are popular when a team is denying and players fade off to receive the ball. Common cuts such as the give-and-go and rear cut are incorporated into many offenses. In the give-and-go a player passes to a teammate and cuts in front of the defense to get the ball back. Rear cut works the same way, except the offensive player cuts behind the defense.

Using the correct pivot foot is important after the ball is caught after a cut. One foot is always down as a pivot foot, while the other is free to move. The free foot should not be behind the pivot foot because it gives the defense a chance to belly up on the offensive player while he is off balance.

Curl Cut

- Curl cuts are used often when a defender is trailing the play and gets caught on a screen. Having a chair in place of a screener is a good way to learn how to curl cut.

- Players should be ready to receive the ball and continue to curl after the screen is set.

- Stepping with the foot closest to the basket allows for a quicker step closer to the screener.

- Passer should pass ball ahead, not behind, receiver.

- The shooter must square to the basket in the motion of a curl cut.

Fade Cut

- Many shooters like the fade cut because it allows them to quickly get a shot off.

- If the defense is denying the ball out to the wing, a fade cut can be used. A player takes a few steps up to wing and fades back.

- The player's hands must be up to show teammates he is open and fading back.

- After the ball is caught, the player should have his knees bent and ready to shoot. Remember that players are fading back to catch the ball, so they need proper balance.

PROPER SPACING
Players can get many open shots and can open shots for teammates

Teaching proper spacing on the court, especially to younger players, is a tough job. As players get older they will naturally learn to space themselves properly and execute given plays. If you watch a basketball game or even a soccer game, for that matter, many young players are all bunched up around the ball. Why does this happen? All players want to touch the ball; they want a chance to score. Therefore, players tend to bunch up around the ball.

Many times the cause of this bunching is the player with the ball, who does not have his head up and doesn't pass to his teammates. No matter how open a teammate might be, the player with the ball will not see him. So what does another player do? He goes to the ball to get a pass or a handoff. Then all of the players start to do the same thing. This lets the defense steal the ball or get into a jump ball situation.

Coaches can eliminate this problem by having players always

Guards on a String

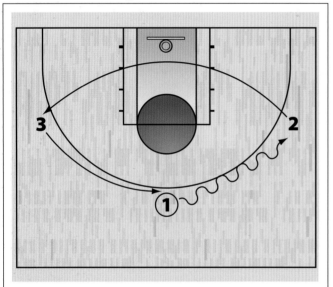

- In this drill, "1" will dribble at "2," who then cuts to the backdoor and goes to the opposite wing.

- The "3" will replace "1" at the top of the key.

Triangle

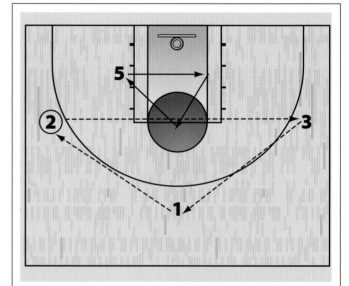

- Here, "2" starts with the ball on the wing. The "5" will post on the ballside block.

- On the skip pass from "2" to "3," the "5" will cut to the opposite block.

- On the pass from "3" to "1," the "5" will cut to the middle of the foul line.

- On the pass from "1" to "2," the "5" will cut to the ballside block.

dribble the ball with their head up. Correcting the mistakes in practice forces players to right their behavior in the game. The rest of the players must always move with a purpose. If they stand and watch, they allow the defense to double team, and players will inevitably start to bunch up again.

Spacing Drill

- The spacing drill allows players to understand spacing and to make use of the triple threat.

- Dribbling is not allowed. Players are spread around the court but paired up, one offensive team and one defensive team.

- Players must get open and pass to teammates. No handoffs are allowed. Passes can be a bounce pass or a chest pass. If the defense steals the ball, or it goes out of bounds, the offense becomes the defense.

- Players must keep the ball alive for two minutes.

Advanced Spacing Drill

- The advanced spacing drill should be done with advanced players. This drill is done the same way as the regular spacing drill. However, after a player passes the ball, he must run and touch the opposite baseline in order to come back into the game.

- Players cannot touch the baseline on the side they passed the ball; instead they must run down to the opposite end to touch the baseline.

- This drill is great for conditioning.

OFFENSE

SCREENS
These overlooked ploys set up scoring opportunities

Maybe the most overlooked ploy in the game of basketball are screens. Screens are constantly being set throughout the game to help players get open. If a screen is done properly, a wide open shot can happen. Teaching your players the right way to set a screen allows them many opportunities to score during a game.

A screen is set when a player initiates a signal on court. For example, a player can raise a fist into the air to let his teammates know that a screen needs to be set. At this time the screener will get into the proper stance.

A screen is performed by having a wide athletic base. Hands are crossed across chest. Players setting screens must establish position first. It's the job of the player coming off the screen to get as close as possible to the screener. A screener's job is to hold his position so the defender runs into him, which allows his teammate to get a shot off or to get open.

Screen Signal

- Besides making eye contact, players can signal for a screen by raising a fist high into the air. This signal allows the offensive players to know a screen will be set.

- Screens can be set anywhere on court. Many screens are set to help players get an open shot.

- Screens can be set to get players open and to free up the dribbler from pressure.

Male Player Screen

- Male players set screens differently than female players. There really is no set way to set a screen other than to have a strong base for players and to have them hold their ground.

- Male players place their arms and hands in a downward manner, crisscrossing their hands below the waist area.

- Don't forget to have your players set screens down low, post to post. Space is limited down low, so players must set a tough screen.

Screens are also set to start an offense to get players open on wing or during an out-of-bounds play. Remind your players that setting a screen is a physical job and that contact will be made with the opponent.

Female Player Screen

- Female players setting screens crisscross their arms across the chest area.

- Players must remember not to bump the opponent with their arms, and they move when the opponent moves.

- Players must realize that an unsuspecting opponent will likely run full speed into them, so it's important to hold their ground.

- Timing is also important. Setting a screen late could result in a foul.

- Double screens can be set with two players side by side.

Player Coming Off Screen

- Players coming off screen, with or without the dribble, should be shoulder to shoulder with the screener so there is no room for the defender to get through.

- Players must read the defensive player when coming off screen. If the defender gets stuck on screen, the player can shoot or drive to the basket.

- If the defender goes behind screen, the player can shoot right away. If the two defensive players switch players they are guarding, then the advantage might be to throw the ball to the tall player with the mismatch.

OFFENSE

111

PICK & ROLL
This ploy can be hard to defend against

After teaching players how to set a screen, the next step is to have the screener roll to the basket. This is called a "pick and roll." The pick and roll is hard to guard if done properly. If your team has a good post and guard, a two-man game can be played often by using the pick and roll.

The pick and roll is done in the same fashion as the screen, except the screener now moves after the teammate uses the screen. The screener signals the play to his teammate by putting his fist into the air. The screen is now set on the side of the defender, about 2 to 3 feet away from the ball handler. The ball handler dribbles to where the screen is set. If the handler can take the ball to the basket and is open, then he should do so. If the handler can't, then he must keep the dribble alive. At this time, the screen rolls toward the basket looking for a pass. When opening up, the screener should seal off the defender to allow for an easy

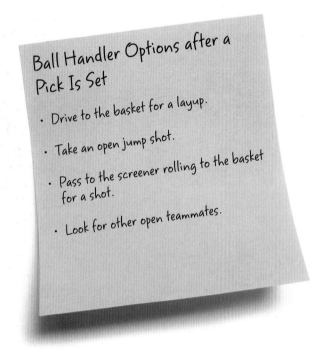

Ball Handler Options after a Pick Is Set

- Drive to the basket for a layup.

- Take an open jump shot.

- Pass to the screener rolling to the basket for a shot.

- Look for other open teammates.

Top of Key Screen

- Screens often take place on top of the key, particularly on the three-point line, because doing so gives the dribbler more of an option to go left or right.

- This type of screen tends to be done by the forward, who sets a screen for a guard to get open.

- If your team has a strong, fast dribbler, this setup will cause many mismatches for teams.

pass. Screeners must open up toward the dribbler, not turn the other way to see the ball.

The screener also has the option of faking the screener slipping the screen. This happens when the screener pretends to set a screen and then quickly cuts to the basket, or the screener sets the screen and, instead of rolling, pops out for a shot.

Pick and rolls create many mismatches and problems for the defense. By spreading out your offense and allowing for pick and rolls to occur during the offense, you also allow for the ball to be kicked out. Both offense and defense must be aware of mismatches if a team switches on screens.

Wing Screen

- In a motion offense, forwards start on wings and come down to set a screen for the guards to get open.

- Guards can also crisscross under the basket and set screens on each other's man.

- Finally, the forward can either come out to a wing and set a screen on the defender so that the wing player can score or do a pick and roll. It's a great way to get a quick hit to score.

Screen and Pop

- As your players progress throughout the season, they should move on to more advanced screen options.

- Screen and pop and slipping screen are two ploys that involve the screen.

- "Slipping screen" means the screener fakes setting a screen and instead rolls right to the basket for the ball.

- "Screen and pop" means the screener sets a screen and doesn't roll; instead she flares out for a jump shot by stepping back.

DRILLS TO INCORPORATE IN OFFENSE

Don't scrimmage just to have your players play but rather make it mean something

When you incorporate an offense or any play being taught to your team, the offensive plays must be taught slowly. Taking each player through the necessary steps allows the other players to understand. Make sure all the players know the different positions. The players on the court can help the others if they get confused about where to go.

Start off running the offense without defense. Run it through several times, making sure players work their way up to game speed. After players understand the play, bring in defense. At this time you will see things change. Players will forget where to go, and options will be closed off by the defense. Players will get frustrated.

Dummy Offense

- "Dummy offense" is a term used to describe players running plays without defense.

- After introducing a play, have five players down at one end of the court and five players down at the other running the play.

- As coach, you should stand in the middle to correct any mistakes. Don't forget to sub in all players.

- If you have an assistant coach, be sure to have her correcting mistakes as well.

Possession Offense

- Possession offense can be run several ways.

- If the offensive team scores, it keeps the ball until the defense can stop it.

- If the defense stops the team, the defense becomes the offense.

- Coaches can also add a fast break if the defensive team steals the ball or gains possession. The defense brings the ball back to the offense, and possession is started again.

- Possessions should start with a check ball from the defense.

Take time again to explain the different options and what to do. If your team still has a hard time with defense, clear the defense off the court and go over the offensive play again until it is understood. Avoid scrimmaging right away when putting in new plays. Instead, run a controlled scrimmage with possessions. Here's a controlled scrimmage example: The offensive team gets the ball five times in a row (regardless of baskets scored). Then the defense players and offense players switch. After a couple of practices, incorporate the learned plays into a full-court scrimmage.

ZOOM

Basketball plays are all about teamwork and execution. Your team can have the best athletes, but if they can't execute a play your team will be in trouble when pitted against a great defensive team. Choosing the proper play against the defense creates more opportunities to score.

Three-on-three

- Playing three-on-three is a great teaching tool to get players to learn to play and pass to each other.

- Three-on-three allows all players to touch the ball. There are no set positions, and players can work on screens and skills.

- Teach players to always catch the ball in the triple threat position. This gives them the option of shooting, passing, or dribbling.

- Three-on-three also works on "on-the-ball defense" and "help defense."

Scrimmage

- Scrimmaging in practice can be done several ways.

- To make scrimmage competitive, mix up teams equally so one team of starters aren't dominating. Make it fun for all.

- Scrimmaging should be done during the last part of practice. Coaches should never scrimmage with players. Coaches are there to instruct.

- Coaches should call all fouls and make scrimmage as game like as possible.

OFFENSE

BASIC OFFENSE: 6–9-YEAR-OLDS

Players should not be pigeon-holed into specific positions at this time of development

Running an offense is pretty much nonexistent at this age level. Instead these younger players should be taught basic skills. However, at some point these young players have to play in a game. Offensively, do not have any structured pattern offenses. First, get players comfortable on court. They will start to figure things out. Your main objective is to get them moving and not standing still. Often the best intentions go by the wayside when young players go onto the court because they don't remember most of the plays.

Teaching a few basic cuts and maybe a screen helps with spacing. Younger players tend to do two things: Act like robots and not move out of the spot the coach puts them in

Motion Offense

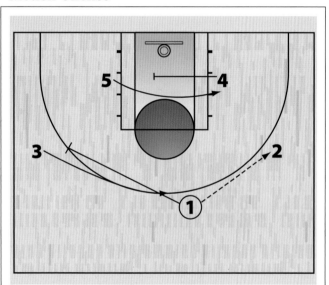

Baseline Runner

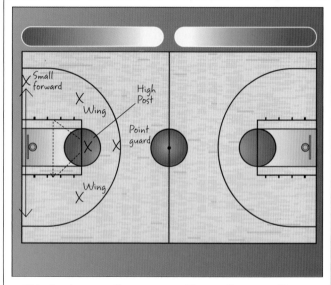

- This offense has good court balance with three perimeter players and two post players. It gives you both inside and outside presence.

- A basic motion offense involves passing, screening, and cutting. The diagram above shows the initial movement.

- On the pass from "1" to "2," several events occur: "4" will cross screen for "5," and "1" will screen across for "3." The "2" can shoot, pass to "5" on the block, or pass to "3" at the top of the key.

- To continue the offense, perform the same movement on opposite side of court.

- This simple zone offense allows for a point guard, two wings and a post, and a player running the baseline.

- The post inside will go from the block to foul line to opposite block and continue a triangle pattern.

- The smaller post will run back and forth on baseline. These two players will move based on where the ball is.

or move around too much and chase the ball, causing players to bunch up. It's your job to find a happy medium.

A motion offense or a one-three-one set is the most basic set to run against a man and zone. Motion offense allows you to teach fundamentals. They have freedom in this offense. Motion offense has three basic rules: After every pass, the player must cut or screen; do not stand still for more than two seconds; and take a shot when open.

Pass and Screen Away

- When teaching pass and screen away to younger players, have two lines set up.

- Divide players into two lines, one on top with the ball, the other in the wing area without the ball. Coach is in the opposite wing.

- The player in the middle passes the ball to the coach and goes to screen for the player in line at the opposite wing. Have a chair there to simulate a defensive player. The player then comes off the screen and cuts to the basket to get a pass from the coach.

Pass and Exchange

- Pass and exchange is an easy way to teach players to move to different spots.

- Players can do this when they pass the ball. They just exchange with the player opposite them.

- For example, point guard passes to the wing and exchanges with the other wing. Post player exchanges with the other post when the ball is passed to their side. This now places players in different positions to repeat the process.

OFFENSE

ZONE DEFENSE

This formation can be easier for younger players to understand

Zone defense is normally played in developmental leagues because it's easier for younger players to understand and it teaches spacing. These zone defense players are responsible for their area. Teams that play zone do so because their opponents can't shoot from the outside, they can't guard them man to man, or they want to front and back a good post player. Zone is not a relaxed defense; it requires just as much running around and responsibility as man to man.

Several zone formations can be taught. The most popular one is the two-three zone defense. Other zone defenses are one-two-two, three-two, and one-three-one. Typically these zone defenses protect the middle and don't extend outside the three-point line. As the ball shifts, so does the defense. Each player is responsible for her area.

Moving outside the designated area will cause the defense to not work. Players must communicate with each other

Two-three

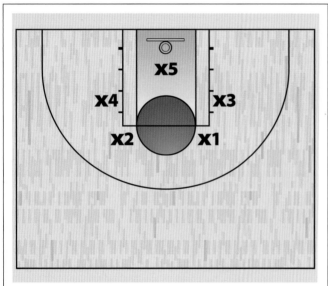

- The X1 and X2 positions are typically smaller guards that play around the elbow area.

- The X5 position is the tallest player, your center.

- The X4 and X3 positions can be a bigger guard and a forward.

- You want your taller player underneath the basket for rebounding.

One-two-two

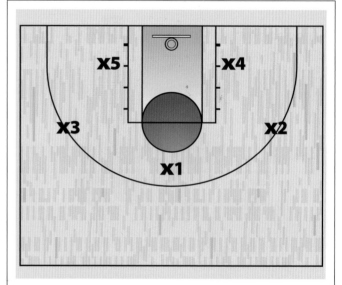

- The advantage of the one-two-two is being able to pressure the ball outside of the arc.

- Allowing for some trapping can be effective against a good outside shooting team.

- The disadvantage of the defense is that the high post area and defense can be attacked from corners.

and close gaps when necessary. When a player's hands are constantly up, it takes away from the space on the court. A rule of thumb for zone defense is to not go outside the three-point line. If a player has to help another player out, the player who is being helped must always release the other back to his spot after he recovers. By doing this, zone defense becomes effective.

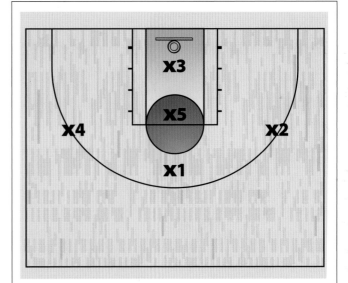

RED ● LIGHT

Younger players have a tendency to move their bodies when the ball is moved around by the offense. They need to be aware that players could be behind them. Stress to them to move their bodies slightly so they can see the ball moving and the players cutting.

DEFENSE

Three-two

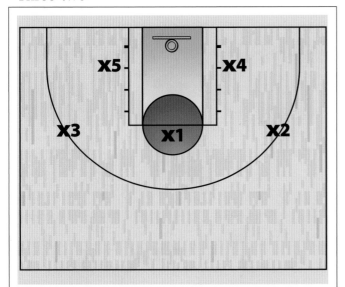

- The three-two zone is commonly used to defend teams with good outside shooting and weaker post players.

- You can use it as a trapping defense.

- X1, X2, and X3 should be your three quickest players because they are expected to make the most defensive movement and slides.

One-three-one Half Court

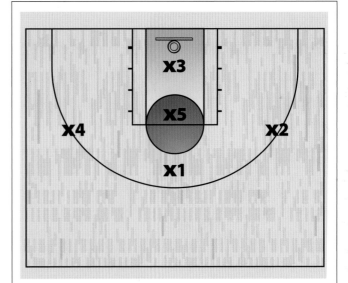

- X1 is the most important player on the court. This player guides the dribbler to a position on the sideline where he can be double teamed.

- The secret of the one-three-one zone press is the double team. The players who are double teamed

usually are not the ones stealing the ball.

- X4 and X2 must drop down to the box area when the ball is in the corner.

- X3 should be a quick baseline defender so he can intercept inside passes. This is the best defense for trapping.

MAN-TO-MAN DEFENSE

This formation is difficult to teach but will allow players to benefit later on

One of the most important rules of defense is to keep the body between the man and the basket and to keep the person being guarded in front of you. The proper defensive stance is this: Feet should be shoulder width apart, knees bent, butt down, back straight, with the player ready on the balls of his feet. A good way to teach this stance is to have players pretend that they are sitting in a chair and that the chair is taken from underneath them. Hands should be outside the knees with palms up. Players must stay low at all times. This low stance allows them to change direction quickly. The second the defensive players stand up is when the offense goes by them.

Team Man Defense

- Team man defense functions only when players talk.

- A big weakness in team man defense comes when screens are set. Coaches must make it clear to players what they are doing, whether it's switching or getting over the top screens.

- The shell drill is excellent for teaching how to rotate and play team defense. Drill is done with four players on defense and four on offense.

- The ball is moved around to each offensive player, no dribbles allowed. Stop play from time to time to ensure defense is in correct position.

Individual Playing Defense

- Man-to-man defense requires each player to guard his man in every defensive situation. The best defensive player usually guards the opponent's best player. When making defensive assignments, match up by size. Then adjustments can be made during the game.

- Typically forwards guard forwards, and guards guard guards.

- Playing man defense requires good peripheral vision by players. Be aware that putting your best player on the opponent's best player might tire your player during the game.

Defensive positioning should be within arm's reach of the person being guarded, so pressure is put on the ball. Focus is on the belly button or numbers on the jersey. Other body parts will move, but the midsection won't. Players should force the opponent to go where he doesn't want to and turn him in the process.

The proper way to move when guarding the dribbler is to step and push off. Players should step sideways with the lead foot, then push off with the other foot to catch up. The feet never leave the floor, and quick slides are necessary.

Face Guarding/Denying

- Face guarding is a ploy used to keep a player from touching the ball. The defensive player does not look at the ball but rather concentrates on the man.

- Face guarding is used at times when a team is pressing man to man.

- It can be successful during a press if the person guarding the ball is back on defense to help. Otherwise, the opposing team will just throw the ball overhead.

- Face guarding can be used when a team plays a box and one.

RED ● LIGHT

Younger players have a tendency to "hug" the person they guard. Remind them that the hand position is actually lower (by the knee area) and that they should not stand up. Emphasize a lower stance to prevent this "hug." These players also tend to cross feet when sliding and to gallop up and down. Teach strong body stance and have players focus on sliding properly to improve in this area.

Basic Defensive Fundamentals

- Have good position.

- Maintain proper stance.

- Execute good footwork.

- Control the body.

- Block the shooting and passing lanes without fouling.

FULL-COURT PRESSURE DEFENSE

The smartest basketball players know the importance of good defense

Tight man-to-man pressure defense can be played full court, three-quarter court, or half court. Full-court pressure defense is most effective when sprung as a surprise or used for short periods. Many teams like to use pressure defense after a made basket because adrenaline is pumping, and it's a good signal to know which defense to go into.

Pressure defense is most effective against teams that have weak ball handlers or are an inexperienced team. If your players are quick and smart, allow them to play pressure defense. Players enjoy this type of defense because it results in quick layups and causes the other team to panic. Also, fans love the up-tempo style.

One-two-one-one Diagram

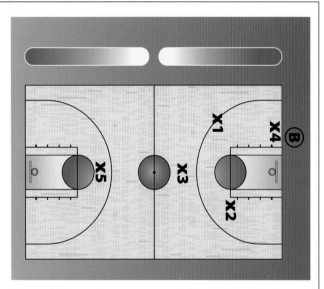

- The one-two-one-one should deny the inbounder's pass; defense should trap the player if the pass is made.

- It should defend the pass back to the inbounder; defense should trap on reverse to the other side; and trap again on the pass up to the sideline.

- Players should sprint back when the press is beaten.

Ball Pressure

- A good defender puts pressure on the ball, whether the player is trying to dribble, pass, or shoot.

- Defenders should have active hands, be able to move quickly, and know the offensive player's strength and weakness.

- Players should never allow an opponent to shoot a ball uncontested. They should be careful not to attempt to block shots all the time because the offense will give a head fake and go around the defensive player. Have players limit their opponent's vision by putting their hands up.

Defensive players play closer than normal to whomever they guard. Players have the option of face guarding if the coach doesn't want the ball inbounded. Defensive players must go after the offensive player in an aggressive manner. Defensive players must "push up on the player" (that is, add pressure) to make sure the player doesn't get by them. Players should force the opponent to dribble with his weak hand. After the ball is picked up by the opponent, defensive players should wave their arms and block the opponent's vision. This defense can allow players to double team and trap all over court. The term "run and jump" refers to this style of play. Advanced players will understand this type of defense, but you may need to start with the basics for younger players.

If your team lacks offensive skills, defense can be easily taught. Good defense is simply a matter of working hard. The technique and manner in which defense is played never change; the individual is assigned a particular player and held responsible for that player.

Trapping

- Trapping is a way for the defense to get a turnover or a quick steal.

- Certain areas on court allow for better traps because the baseline and sidelines act as another defender.

- Trapping is done by two players guarding the person with the ball.

- The best spots to trap are near the sideline and right over half court. Players should not trap in midcourt because there's too much space for movement and opportunity.

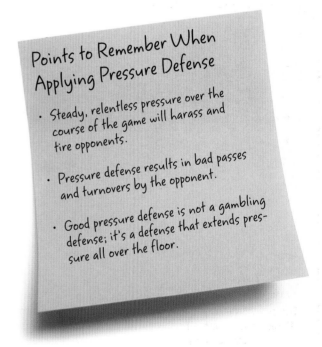

Points to Remember When Applying Pressure Defense

- Steady, relentless pressure over the course of the game will harass and tire opponents.

- Pressure defense results in bad passes and turnovers by the opponent.

- Good pressure defense is not a gambling defense; it's a defense that extends pressure all over the floor.

HELP DEFENSE

Getting all players to talk on defense is often the hardest job for a coach

Help defense, or weak side defense, is critical for stopping the other team. When a player beats another player or when a player gets caught on a screen, some type of help or weak side defense must be used. Communication is the key to help defense.

When a player plays a man not directly involved in the current play, he needs to be ready to help a teammate who gets beat. The person in help defense shouldn't be denying the ball or looking at his man; instead he should be about two steps away from his opponent so he can see both the ball play and his man. In practice, have players point to the ball and the player they are guarding. Help defense players

Team Help Defense

- In order to play help defense, players must see the ball at all times.

- Teach players to point at the ball and their opponents and then to use their peripheral vision to see both.

- When a player calls for help, quick reaction is key to

helping out. Players must act immediately.

- Have faith in your players to recover after helping their teammates out.

- Jumping to the ball instead of staring at an opponent puts players in position to help.

Players in Help Defense

- Players in help defense need to know when to rotate properly.

- If a player is one pass away from the action, he denies the ball.

- Two passes away means the player needs to have one foot in the lane so he is

close enough to help and to get back to his own player.

- As the ball is passed to different areas of the court, adjustments should be made. Players will apply ball pressure, deny, and play help defense at various points in the game.

should be aligned in the center of the court and be ready to step back until the teammate can recover.

Make sure players jump to the ball when it is passed. Making quick adjustments instead of simply standing still allows players to react and be in a better position for the next movement. Jumping to the ball allows players to get in front of cutters, avoid screens, and help their teammate. These actions should be done quickly. Recovery is a must; players should rush back to their man or position.

ZOOM

Another defensive strategy that involves helping is called "doubling down." This strategy occurs when a good low post player gets the ball. The perimeter player goes down and double teams the opponent, making it difficult for the post player to move and therefore forcing him to throw the ball back out.

Helping with a Screen

- There are two ways to help when a screen is set. Hedging out in front of an offensive player to slow him down, and yelling "switch" if you want to switch guarding a player with a teammate.

- Communicating and yelling "screen" make the defensive player aware of the play.

- If the player is a good shooter, the defense must go on top of the screen. A teammate will help by hedging out to slow the opponent down, allowing the player to get through.

Rules of Help Defense

- Always communicate.

- Follow where the ball is at all times.

- Be in position to help.

- Keep track of your own man.

- Act immediately.

125

CLOSE OUT
Players should contest all shots and close all gaps when on defense

Closing out a player can be performed anywhere on court. This simply means that when a player comes from a distance to play his man, he usually is in a sprint to recover. When this happens, to slow himself down the player uses quick, choppy stutter steps to close out an offensive player. The defensive player is now in a good position to stay in front of the player they are guarding.

Defensive players must stay low and in control. They must avoid running past an offensive player and standing up during a close out. The stutter step allows players to stay in front of the offensive player. Closing out can happen on a skip pass or when the ball "swings" around the zone. Players can practice closing out when playing one-on-one in practice. A great drill for this, called "one-on-one close out," can be done in different positions on the floor.

After the defense closes out the player, the player is in a

Closing Out

- To train players on closing out, have all players line up horizontally on the baseline.

- The first group of six players will act after the whistle is blown. Players sprint straight. When the whistle blows again, players will "chop it out" by stuttering with their feet and bringing their arms slightly above the shoulder area.

- Another blow of the whistle signals the players to sprint again. And yet another whistle blow has them stutter step.

- This process is repeated up and down the court.

Close-out Team

- This drill incorporates closing out and sliding. This can also be used during warm-ups before a game.

- Coach stands with the ball at the elbow area. The team lines up directly in front of the coach on the baseline.

- The first player sprints midway and then chops out until the player reaches the coach with the ball. The player then slides to the sideline, back pedals to the end of the baseline, then slides the length of the baseline to the opposite corner.

- The next player repeats the process.

ready defensive stance. If the player being guarded is weak when dribbling left (the majority of players are), then the defensive player should force the opponent to his left. To do this, the defensive player's left foot should be forward, and the body should angle the offensive player to his left. This allows the defensive player possibly to get a steal or make the dribbler pick up the ball. The opposite is true for a left-handed player—the right foot should be forward and the body angled to force the opponent to his right.

Close outs and other defensive strategies work best when there is a lot of communication. Train your players to talk all the time on the court, building team defense. Verbally signaling to teammates when opponents come down the court aids in help defense, close outs, and more. Communication should be reinforced in practice and all basketball terms understood.

Closing Gaps

- Closing gaps is important for good defense, especially when a team is playing a zone.

- Closing gaps prevents the offensive players from getting through the zone.

- Gaps can be closed by two players with both of their feet touching to prevent the offensive player from getting to the lane.

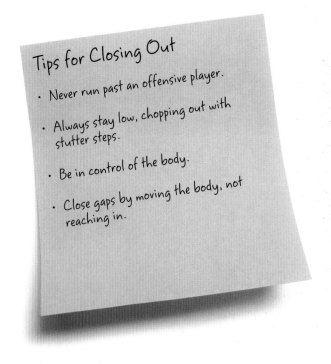

Tips for Closing Out

- Never run past an offensive player.

- Always stay low, chopping out with stutter steps.

- Be in control of the body.

- Close gaps by moving the body, not reaching in.

127

DENYING BALL

This ploy can push the offense farther and farther out

A good defensive basketball team does not let opponents touch the ball. Denying the ball from the offense and not allowing the offense to set up its play result in a scramble by the other team and steals from the defense. Most offenses begin with a pass to the wing player. Denying the ball pushes the offense farther and farther out. Offenses want to start within range of a good shot, preferably by the three-point line. Defenses that are successful in denying the ball on the wing force the offense to move farther out to receive a pass.

Denying the ball is done simply by having the arm up in the passing lanes between the ball and the person being guarded. Players shouldn't overextend or get too close to the opponent, who then could go through the backdoor. Players must drop their bodies when the offensive players drop.

Denying the ball can be used throughout the game. However, it is used many times when the defense is trying to

Denying Ball Stance

- When teaching younger players to deny the ball, remind them that the arm closest to ball should always be up in the passing lanes.

- When a player has the opportunity to steal, he must go after the ball with the passing-lane hand. Younger players tend to go after the ball with the opposite hand, which can result in players going through the backdoor or missing the ball.

- Players should be in an athletic stance and slide, not looking at the player; peripheral vision is critical in denial defense.

Denying the Wing

- Denying the wing results in a lot more work than denying the post because guards have more space to work.

- Denying the wing requires quick, intense steps.

- It can result in many steals and creates an up-tempo style of play. Players enjoy this, but the play can be tiring.

- Well-conditioned teams can sustain pressure defense throughout game, whereas younger players tire easily. Coaches should make decisions about denying based on the team.

get the ball back after a made basket, when an opponent is inbounding the ball, or when the defense is trying to deny the better players the ball.

Denying Post

- Whether a player is guarding the post at the high or low post area, denying the pass from the side is necessary.

- Remember this: The side the ball is on is the side on which the defensive player should position her body in a denial stance, with the arm up in the passing lane.

- The defense position changes based on the offensive team moving the ball.

- Help will come from the weak side if the ball is thrown over the head.

Post Defense

- Post defense can be played by fronting the post. This means the defensive player fights to get in front of the offensive player so the ball cannot be passed down low. Fronting the post results in a constant fight for position. Defense should avoid contact by moving around to not be pinned by offense.

- If the defense can't get into position, make sure the offensive player doesn't back down the defense too far.

- By establishing a wide, strong base and pushing the forearm into the opponent's back, the defense prevents the opponent from backing down.

BASIC DEFENSE: 6–9-YEAR-OLDS

Switching from man to zone strategies from time to time allows beginner players to learn both

Teaching beginner players how to play defense can be difficult, but teaching them the right way is important. Youth sports are supposed to develop players for higher levels of basketball, so teaching both man and zone defense is recommended. There are positives and negatives to teaching beginner players zone defense: Teaching zone at this age could develop bad habits that won't work as the level of competition gets stronger. As players get older, man-to-man defense is mostly what is played. The positive of playing zone is that it teaches proper spacing and doesn't require much thought. It's easier for these younger players to understand. The negative of teaching man defense at this level is that

Two-three Zone

- A two-three zone is played by many developmental teams.

- It is the easiest zone that can be taught and learned.

- Typically small guards take up the two elbow spots, and the three taller players make up the three bot-tom positions, two blocks and a middle person (thus, two-three zone). The tallest player on the team plays middle.

- The zone shifts as the ball shifts, and defensive hands are always up. Remember that communication is a must.

Area of Two-three Zone

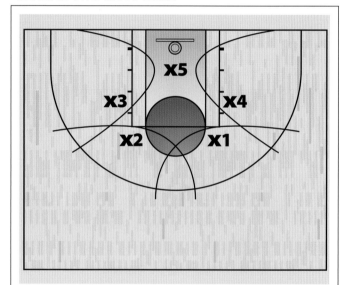

- These areas are covered by players in a two-three zone.

- Players are responsible for a certain area.

- They can help out in other areas as well, but they must get back to their "assigned" area.

players can get so consumed with whom they guard that they tend to follow the person around. Help defense is never seen here, and players don't get the ball because the defensive player is practically hugging them. The positive of man defense is that young players eventually must learn how to play man, so they're being set up well. Youth coaches should focus on the technical part and correct mistakes until players get old enough to understand man concepts.

Switching up the defense and incorporating both man and zone allow younger players to develop. For example, play just man-to-man defense for one quarter, then zone defense the next. As players get older, particularly at thirteen and fourteen years old, switching up the defense can be incorporated after a made basket. This concept needs to be practiced so players aren't confused and reminded all the time by the coach.

Practicing man-to-man concepts should start with basics on the ball, then denying the ball, and finally help defense. Be sure players understand each concept before moving on to the next.

Half-court Man

- When your team is playing half-court man, match players up according to opponents' size, skill, and quickness. Depending on the strength of the opposing team, certain players are played differently.

- Someone who is a good shooter should always be played with a hand up. An opponent who can't dribble too well should be pressured all the time.

- Some leagues require teams to drop back and play only half court until the last quarter or last two minutes of play. At this time the team can play full-court man.

Shell Drill

- This drill practices proper defensive positioning and movement as the ball moves.

- Five defensive players guard five offensive players: One player on top of the key, two wings, and two players in opposite corners. Offense is also on the court.

- The ball is passed around the perimeter. Defense moves, practicing proper positioning.

- The drill is done slow at first to check proper defensive positions. As players understand, speed up the tempo.

BASIC TECHNIQUE
Boxing out will stop opponents from getting the ball

Rebounding is one of the most important aspects of winning basketball games. There are two types of rebounding: Defensive rebounding and offensive rebounding. Defensive rebounding completes good defense and limits teams to one shot. Offensive rebounding gives teams extra opportunities to score after a missed shot.

Good rebounders are a must to a team. Without good rebounders, teams will struggle. The first important rule of rebounding is to get the inside position and box out. The term "box out" means to make contact with the person being guarded to seal him away from the hoop and away from the ball.

First, a player makes contact with the player being guarded. He pivots with either the left or right foot in between the opponent's legs. He keeps the body position bent and arms up and out. A common term, "butt in the gut," is an easy way

Boxing Out Position

- The keys to rebounding are positioning and concentration on the ball. Players should anticipate the flight of the ball. They should make contact with the player they are guarding or the player in the area. Players should hold the box out long enough to go after the ball.

- Players should avoid offensive players pushing from behind. This causes players to get too far under the basket. Make sure that hands are up.

- Players should jump up and grab rebounds in a strong, controlled manner.

Team Boxing Out

- Team boxing out requires everyone to do his job. Whether it's man-to-man or zone defense, all players are responsible for boxing out.

- A good boxing-out team will actually box out so well that the ball can take a bounce on the floor. This is called "clearing."

- Players need to communicate and help each other by yelling "Box" when a shot goes up.

- Failure of a player to box out can result in a lost ball.

for younger players to remember this concept. As the opponent moves to get to the basket, have players move with him, keep an eye on the ball, and rebound when it comes off of the basket.

Defensive players must aggressively go after the ball once the opponent is boxed out. Jumping high with both hands to grab the ball and to rip it down ensures a good rebound. After the ball is in hands, players protect it by pivoting away from opponents with elbows out and the ball around the chin area or above the head. Doing this allows players to find an open guard to start a fast break or to bring the ball up to start the offense.

Offensive rebounding allows players to be aggressive and to go after missed shots. Players must be quick on their feet and get an inside position on the defender. Players should assume that every shot will be missed. After the ball is offensively rebounded, players must go up strong and power it back up to the basket, usually shooting the ball off the backboard.

Jumping for Rebound

- Younger players have a tendency to wait for the rebound.

- They must be reminded to go after the ball by jumping up and getting it, not waiting for the ball to come into their hands.

- Advanced players will be able to jump higher, but jumping high doesn't mean they are great rebounders.

- Boxing out first is critical. Then jumping high to get the ball will complete the rebounding process.

Chinning Ball

- After rebounding, stance is important. An athletic stance allows the rebounder to get the ball to a guard.

- The ball is held in the chin area with elbows out. A wide, strong base allows a player to pivot in a controlled manner without walking.

- The ball can now be thrown over the head as an outlet pass.

- The ball should be kept high so that no tie-ups occur.

INDIVIDUAL REBOUNDING DRILLS
Rebounding is every player's responsibility

Getting good position and anticipating missed shots are key to rebounding. The ball is more likely to be missed opposite from where the shot was taken. For players to become better rebounders, they must learn several things. Players must know proper technique, must be aggressive, must get inside position, and must be determined to go after the ball. Having height and good jumping abilities does have its advantages in rebounding; however, proper rebounding technique and

aggressiveness will win over height in the long run.

One of the biggest mistakes younger players make is to watch the flight of the ball instead of positioning themselves to get the rebound. Players must find an opponent to box out first and then get the ball.

Drills that focus on individual rebounding should be taught first. After each player masters the rebounding skill, then it's easier to teach rebounding. Boxing out on the foul line should

Younger Players Boxing Out

- This is a great drill for beginner players learning to box out while matching their opponent's movements.

- Players partner up around the court. Coach blows the whistle to have a player box out his partner. This is repeated so both players

box out five times, each taking turns.

- Then all boxed-out players should move three steps to their right when you blow the whistle. Again each player boxes out five times. In the next turn, players move three steps to the left.

Jumping for the Ball

- This simple drill teaches young players to jump, pivot, and conquer their fear of the ball.

- Players line up behind each other. Coach throws the ball straight up into the air to one player, who jumps up and catches it.

- After the player lands, he must "chin ball" and pivot around. He continues pivoting until told to stop. Then the next player goes.

- Middle-aged players can do this drill, but the ball is thrown off of the backboard from different spots on the floor.

KNACK COACHING YOUTH BASKETBALL

be taught separately from individual and team rebounding. Boxing out on a foul shot is done differently and needs to be taught so players aren't confused.

Teach both defensive and offensive rebounding. Many drills will develop both at the same time. Having rewards or penalties for players during rebounding drills allows for more aggressive play on both ends. While defensive players work on boxing out, offensive players should try to get inside position as well. Offensive players will work extra hard by trying to move quickly around the person boxing them out. This then forces the defensive player to be more aggressive. A win-win situation is now created. Practices for younger players should focus more on jumping up and grabbing the ball.

Circle Boxing Out

- This drill teaches boxing out and sealing players from touching the ball.

- Two players stand on the center circle with the ball in the middle, one player on defense, and the other on offense. The offensive player tries to touch the ball, while the defensive player tries to prevent this from happening by sliding with the player and pushing him out in a box-out formation.

- This drill teaches both players to be aggressive and makes defensive players hold the box out.

Offensive Rebounding

- This drill works on jumping and going back up for the shot.

- Form one line of players. Throw a ball off of the backboard. The first player jumps to get the ball and goes back up with a shot. The player will either go back up strong or take a dribble to get into a better position.

- The player determines if he needs a dribble based on where the rebound goes.

- Move line to different areas of the court and throw the ball off of the backboard at different angles.

EAM REBOUNDING DRILLS

Team rebounding builds team chemistry—all players are held accountable

Team rebounding is critical for winning games. All players must be responsible for boxing out their opponent. If all players do their job, good team rebounding is possible. The technique for team rebounding is the same as for individual rebounding, but there will be times when players will have to box out their opponent in a certain area. Many younger teams play zone defense, which will then require them to box out different players. As players advance, man-to-man defense is taught and played more, making these players responsible for guarding a specific opponent. As individual rebounding improves, team rebounding will improve.

Some important team rebounding strategies should be

Triangle Rebounding Drill

- This is a great rebounding drill that simulates real-game situations.

- Setup: Three players are on offensive, three on defense, one at the foul line, the other two in corners just outside the key. Defensive players form a triangle facing the offense. Defensive

players slide in a triangle pattern while the offense stands still.

- Toss the ball off the backboard. At this time defensive players must find one of the offensive players to box out in their area.

Crashing Boards

- Form two even lines of players at the elbows facing the basket, matched up by height. Coach starts with the ball in the middle. Two players start the drill.

- Throw the ball directly into the middle of the backboard, making sure the ball hits hard. At this time both

players attack the boards to get the ball. The player who secures the rebound earns points for his team.

- Players can box each other out and chase after the ball until it is recovered. Repeat for the next set.

done throughout the game: Try to establish a triangle of players around the basket, one player on each side of the hoop and one in front. Players must be careful to not get too far under the rim because opponents must be boxed out away from the basket. Always have weak side rebounding. This means that when a shot is up, make sure players are positioned on the opposite side of the shot.

Finally, long rebounds are seen a lot when teams shoot three-pointers. Guards should be aware of this. Long rebounds will go over players boxing out on the inside, so it's necessary for guards to box out. Boxing out as a team allows the defense to regain possession of the ball and transition the team to offense. This starts a fast break.

Younger players have a hard time understanding the boxing-out concept. Instead they all go for the ball after it's shot. They also tend to hold the ball in a crouch position, which causes many jump balls throughout the game. Teach players to use the pivot foot to get away from opponents and to create space to find an open player.

Eleven

- This game is played to eleven with each basket worth one point. Form a line of players on the baseline. Three players go at one time.

- Throw the ball off the backboard. Players fight to get the rebound. When a player gets the rebounds, she can go back up to try to score. The other two players play defense on this person.

- If a player scores, she goes to the back of the line, and the next player jumps into the drill.

Possession Rebounding

- This drill involves the whole team at one time. Players partner up around the three-point line. Defense faces offense, matching up by height.

- Throw the ball off the backboard from different spots on the floor so different players can rebound the ball.

- If the defense gets the rebound, it gets a point. If the offense gets the rebound, then the defense has to sprint up and down the court. Then the players repeat the drill until they get five total points.

137

OUTLET PASS

A good rebounder will outlet the ball to start a fast break to score

The outlet pass is an important component of rebounding. After the rebound is made, players need to pull the rebound into the chin area with elbows out. This concept is called "chinning the ball." This allows players to squeeze the ball, pivot away from defense, and protect the ball. Make sure players do not swing their elbows, which will cause a flagrant foul to the opponent.

At this point players can move the ball overhead to get ready to throw an outlet pass. Be careful that the ball doesn't go behind the head, which will allow an opponent to slap the ball from behind. Keeping the ball overhead allows for a better pass to be made and prevents opponents from taking it. The ball should never be brought down past the head area when rebounding. Players shouldn't cover it with their body, which can create a jump ball situation and also slows down the fast break. The body should be positioned in a wide

Technique of Outlet Pass

- Outlet passes are thrown quickly and accurately to get a transition game going. Hands should be on the side of the ball for added force.

- Outlet drills are performed off a rebound.

- A bad outlet pass can lead to many turnovers and easy baskets for opponents because they steal the ball right from under and next to their basket.

Footwork

- Pivoting away from defense is important in rebounding. When a player pivots, one foot remains on the floor while the other foot steps around to find an open player.

- Pivoting toward the defense creates jump ball situations and slows down

making the outlet pass and getting a fast break. Avoid this type of play.

- Pivoting creates space and allows for accurate passing.

- Younger players will sometimes walk after getting the rebound. Be sure to eliminate this bad habit.

stance and pivot away from the defense to give an outlet pass to the guard.

An outlet pass is a strong, accurate, fast pass. Both hands are placed on the side of the ball, allowing force behind the pass. The player should step to the person receiving the ball. Rebounders should never rebound and turn inside toward defenders. They should always rebound and step outward away from defenders. If a rebounder can't get the ball to a teammate, it's okay for the rebounder to dribble a few times to escape pressure. He must dribble with a purpose and find guards. However, remind rebounders not to put the the ground often.

Younger players can perform the outlet pass. They must be reminded to get rid of the ball quickly and not to walk. Emphasize pivoting outward away from defense and throwing an accurate pass.

Outlet Drill

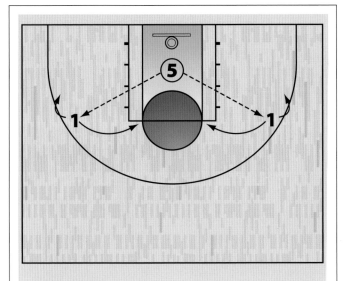

- The "1" will receive the outlet pass from the rebounder inside the three-point line, ball side.

- The player receiving the outlet pass can move right or left.

Foul Line Boxing Out

- Boxing out on the foul line is important so extra chances aren't gained by the opponent.

- The ball must hit the rim before players can box out.

- Taller players are usually placed in the lowest two spaces closest to the basket.

- When boxing out, players have the foot as close to the opponent as possible so they can easily slide across.

- The rebounders in the top two lanes must communicate. One should box out the shooter, and the other should go to the lane area to get the rebound.

CONDITIONING DRILLS

Take a lot of pride in good offensive rebounding; it takes a lot of work

How do you teach players to pick off loose balls that come off missed shots from opponents or teammates? It takes an extra effort to establish good rebounding position. Practicing conditioning-style rebounding drills allows players to train their mind and bodies to continue to go after rebounds. Good offensive rebounding requires determination. Teach

your players to go after every loose ball. Sometimes making more opportunities to score requires toughness.

On many occasions offensive rebounders have to go up strong two or three times to put the ball into the basket. This results in players getting fouled. A nice ending to an offensive rebound, however, is to get fouled while still making the

Superman

- The Superman drill is a conditioning individual drill and is done for thirty seconds or a minute. It requires strength, quickness, and conditioning.

- Player starts outside of the lane area, tosses the ball to the opposite side of the backboard and must slide

- over and catch the ball outside of the lane by jumping up and grabbing it. After it is caught, the player tosses ball to other side. Drill continues.

- Advanced players should be able to do this drill. They must jump outside of the lane lines.

Taps at Basket

- Players divide themselves into groups of six standing in a line at their basket. The first player in line starts with a ball. It is tossed off the backboard. The player then runs in, jumps up for it, catches it, and then taps it off the backboard for the next player in line.

- The next person in line should run in and prepare to jump. The drill continues with players getting back in line.

- If middle-aged players can't tap the ball, just have them throw it off the backboard, catch, and throw back up for the next player.

basket because the player maximizes scoring opportunities.

Some simple reminders can help players become good offensive rebounders. If the defense player isn't boxing out when the shot is up, players should immediately attack the basket. If the player boxes out, try using a reverse spin off the back to get in the front position. Lastly, if players are side by side when a defensive arm is raised, the offensive player can hook the arm by pushing it over his, forcing both arms to drop. Then the offensive player can slide his body in front. Tipping the ball is always an option if a player can't get in front for position. Tipping to oneself or a teammate allows the ball to stay alive.

Younger players going in for offensive rebounds should be careful of going over another player's back. The violation "reaching over the back" occurs when an offensive player grabs the ball out of the hand of the defense from behind. If the defense has established position, the offensive player will be called on this violation by the referee.

Backboard Taps

- This is another timed individual conditioning drill.

- It strengthens calf muscles and allows the player to develop quick jumps when going back up to the basket.

- Start with the player holding the ball above his head. The player continuously jumps up and down, simulating tapping the backboard or hitting the bottom of the net.

- The ball must stay above the head at all times and in hand. After thirty seconds are up, the player shoots a layup and then switches sides.

Full-court Taps

- This is a great team conditioning drill. It is done exactly the same as stationary taps, However, it is now a full-court rebounding drill, which means that instead of going to the back of the line, players must run down court to the opposite line, which is also tapping.

- Both lines start on the right side of the basket (at both ends of the court). After the player taps, he runs down court.

- The ball should never touch the ground. If it does, the drill starts over until it is successfully completed in one minute.

141

TWO-ON-ZERO

Players use a chest pass to get the ball up the floor, then a bounce pass for a layup

The two-on-zero fast break is a great introduction to running a fast break. Start with the basics by having younger players slide down court and pass, which helps them to understand the movement of getting down the court. These drills also emphasize passing and receiving on the move.

A two-on-zero drill should start off using various passes without shooting. Players will pair up and focus on calling names and sliding even with their partner. After this is mastered, introduce the layup. Advanced players will be able to start right away with the layup. This drill should not take long for them.

After players understand the concept of sliding equally

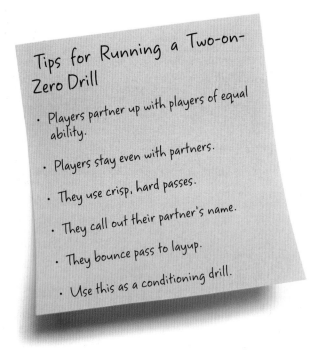

Tips for Running a Two-on-Zero Drill

- Players partner up with players of equal ability.
- Players stay even with partners.
- They use crisp, hard passes.
- They call out their partner's name.
- They bounce pass to layup.
- Use this as a conditioning drill.

Passing Back and Forth

- This drill is used for all age groups. It is a good introduction to a fast break; however, it can be used at anytime for conditioning.

- Players line up with a partner on the baseline in the middle of the court. Partners pass to each other sliding up court. After they get to half court, a new group starts going. No shooting takes place.

- Eventually move the drill to running and then change passes. Make sure players call names out and give good passes. If the ball drops, make them do it again.

KNACK COACHING YOUTH BASKETBALL

with a partner and passing forward, not behind, incorporate the players running down court, not sliding. Make sure that players stay in the middle of the court and that the partner doesn't get too far away or too far up court. A good rule of thumb is to use the distance of the lane line and have players stay that distance between each other. As players approach the basket, one player will have to move in to shoot a layup. A bounce pass must be performed. This drill is great for getting players to talk and for getting younger players to catch the ball on the run. Change passes every few times down court.

Outlet into Two-on-zero

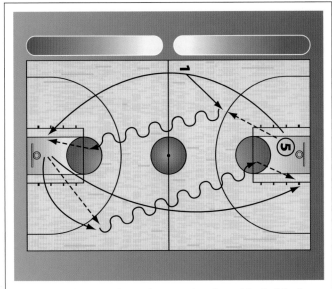

- Two even lines are formed, one under the basket, and the other line in the wing area. Player starts with ball under basket and outlets ball to player in wing area.

- Player in wing gets ball and dribbles to opposite foul line, jump stops, and bounce passes to player

that threw him ball for lay up. The player that makes the lay up continues to run to opposite wing.

- Passer gets rebound, passes to shooter who now dribbles to opposite foul line, then runs behind passer to get pass down other end for a layup.

Passing to Cutter

- When a player passes to a player cutting to the basket, the pass must be made leading the player to the basket.

- A controlled bounce pass is suggested on a fast break.

- The player passing should jump stop at the foul line and not past this point.

- The player should avoid passing the ball behind the receiver and call for the ball.

- The receiver should have a target hand out to catch the ball. Right side should have the right hand out; left side should have the left hand out.

THREE-MAN WEAVE

The rule of thumb never changes: Pass and go behind

The three-man weave can be done several ways. As players advance, these variations can be incorporated. Three-man weave is an excellent conditioning and passing drill. It helps players to develop good hand-eye coordination and to get a feel for their teammates on the court. All players must be in sync for the drill to be executed correctly.

Players form three lines on the baseline with the ball in the middle. The player in the middle passes to either the right or left side. Players in outside lines should start slightly ahead of the middle line. After the ball is passed, the player must follow the pass and go behind the receiver. This player then passes the ball to the opposite player and runs behind that player. As this happens, all players must move up court.

This continues until the ball is down court and bounce passed for a layup. The ball should never touch the ground. No dribbling is allowed except that the player who shoots

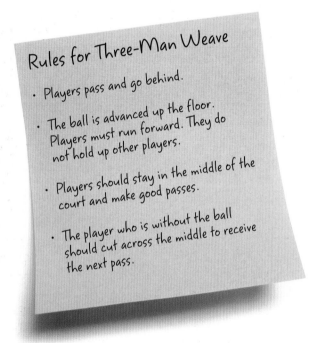

Rules for Three-Man Weave

- Players pass and go behind.

- The ball is advanced up the floor. Players must run forward. They do not hold up other players.

- Players should stay in the middle of the court and make good passes.

- The player who is without the ball should cut across the middle to receive the next pass.

Weave to Two-on-one

- Players start with a regular three-man weave down court. The player who shoots the ball must run back on defense against the two other players who were in the weave.

- This drill teaches playing transition defense and pushing the ball down court.

- As the drill progresses, have players take out a ball to simulate reacting to a made basket and getting the ball up the floor quickly.

KNACK COACHING YOUTH BASKETBALL

the layup might need a dribble to get closer.

When teaching this drill to younger players, remind them they must move forward up the court. You will see they have a tendency to move backward and not go behind the person they passed to. By doing this drill being close together and handing the ball to each other, they will understand the pattern. After this is understood, then have players spread out. Three-man weave can be used with different passes and used as a conditioning drill.

When doing it as a conditioning drill, players go up and down court for a certain amount of time. Remind players that the person who shoots the ball must continue to run to the opposite side to be able to go down the other end. The rebounder will be the person who did not shoot or pass.

Have players form three lines on the baseline with the ball in the middle.

Advanced Three-man Weave

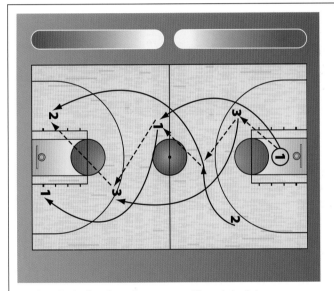

- After the ball is shot, the player runs to the opposite three point line and touches it.

- The person that doesn't shoot or pass gets the rebound first and passes to the person coming in for a layup.

- The original shooter gets the rebound and passes to the original rebounder.

- This results in all three players shooting.

Three-on-zero Fast Break

- The player with the ball passes to either side. Ball is passed back, then middle player passes to other side. This back-and-forth continues until middle player reaches just above three-point line and jump stops at foul line. The two wing players cut into the basket to receive ball for a layup.

- The middle player gets the rebound, and the wings crisscross to go down the other end.

- Wings must stay wide and run hard in lanes. Middle line has a choice to pass to either side. Middle line may use a dribble if needed to get to the foul line.

DEFENSIVE TRANSITION
Players must run back quickly and communicate who has the ball

The term "transition" in basketball can mean two things. A fast break, or offensive transition, is the process of changing from offense to defense. The opposite is changing from offense to defense, or transition defense.

Playing a transition defense can be as simple as having one guard run back after a score, steal, or rebound, and then the rest of the team runs back; or two players run back and get set in a tandem defense to stop a fast break. Tandem defense

is one player (typically the first person back) positioned on the foul line and the other player directly behind but closer to the basket.

The goal of defensive transition is to prevent the opponent from scoring an easy layup. Coach should designate a player to always run back. The player who is told to go back must sprint to the three-point line and then back pedal to the middle of the lane. Sprinting first allows the player to get down fast, then

One Player

- When one player is always sent back on defense, this player's job is to slow down a break.

- The player should position herself in the middle of the key area. The player should not commit completely to the dribbler; instead she should take small jabs and

- fakes at the offense like she is coming out at them.

- The defense wants the offense to shoot a jump shot, which is a lower percentage shot and could result in a missed basket.

Tandem

- Tandem defensive players are also in the key area. One player is at the foul line, the other directly behind but in front of the basket.

- The first person in tandem stops the ball by yelling "Ball." As the ball is passed, the bottom player comes out, and the front player

- then drops all the way down to the level of the offensive player.

- The first player back stops the ball, and the other player quickly runs behind to get set in a tandem.

turn around and play defense. The rest of the team should hustle down court to help players who are back. The job of the back players is to slow down the break until help arrives.

Players might find themselves in a situation against a two-on-one or a three-on-two. Obviously the defense is at a disadvantage. In these situations the defense must stop the layup first. Defensive players must drop as low as the offense. Committing to the ball allows offensive players to pass to a teammate. Defense must stay in the middle and slow down the break. Defense wants the offense to pull up for a jump shot. It's a lower percentage shot, and the player will avoid getting a foul. A three-on-two situation allows another defensive player to help. The top player must stop the ball.

Beating Man to Spot

- There are times when the offensive player beats the defensive player down court. If that happens, the defensive player must spring ahead of the opponent. This move is called "beating man to spot."

- Many younger players tend to run alongside an offensive player to try to catch up to him. This results in a foul because their arms are practically hugging the offensive player.

- Instead teach players to spring ahead and then turn to play defense instead of riding the offensive player.

Transition Sprints

- Transition sprints work on getting back on defense.

- Players line up in two lines on the baseline. Coach blows the whistle. Both players take off and sprint down court to the three-point line and then back pedal off court with their hands above their heads. The next group then goes on the whistle.

- This drill teaches players to sprint back first and then back pedal to see the ball.

147

THREE-ON-TWO

A fast break should be purely instinctual; it should be a reaction to the other team's defense

The three-on-two transition drill can be done in different ways. It can be done coming out of a five-man weave or done basically by having two defensive players already down court. Whichever way you choose to do this drill, several rules must be followed to ensure proper spacing. There should always be a player with the ball in the middle of the floor and two wings. The person dribbling is typically a guard, but allowing different players to dribble up court allows them to handle the ball and improve their dribbling skills. The two wings must get up court quickly. Passing the ball around allows for an open shot because of the advantage of having three players against two. Faking a pass and skipping

Three-on-two Set

- First practice the defense rotation by having two players at a time rotate when the ball is passed. Have three stationary players as offense. When the ball is caught, stop to check defense position. All players on the team should go slowly through the defense rotation.

- Next have two players on defense down at the other end of the court. The three offensive players run down and play against two defensive players.

- Have same defensive players play until everyone goes and then switch up defense. Repeat the process.

Advanced Three-on-two

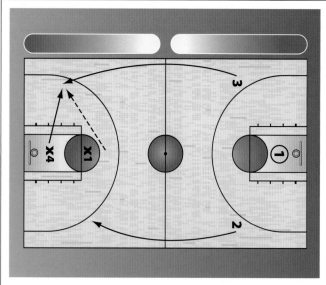

- Player 1 can dribble down the court with the ball or pass it. Players 3 and 2 run wide lanes, while X1 and X4 are in a tandem defense.

- X1 stops the ball and X4 is responsible for the next pass. Player 1 passes to 3 and cuts to the elbow.

- Whoever shoots the ball sprints back on defense. The two defenders rebound the ball and become offensive players, going down the floor two on one.

a ball will throw off the defense. The three-on-two must be done quickly because more time wasted gives the defense a chance to recover.

When the middle player passes to the wing, he should flash to the elbow. This makes it hard for the defense to guard because the top person drops to back, and the back person plays defense on the wing person. This spot creates a gap and an opportunity for an open shot. The opposite wing should then go down to the block to receive a pass or get in position for a layup.

Advanced Three-on-two

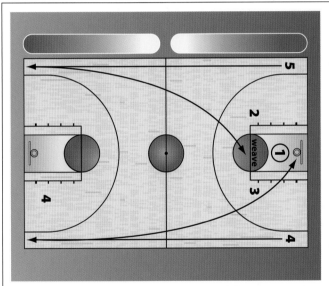

- The drill begins with five lines on the baseline. The outside lines (lines 4 and 5) sprint to the opposite baseline and return to the foul lane area in a tandem.

- Meanwhile, lines 1, 2, and 3 weave down the middle of the court to shoot a layup.

- They rebound the ball and come back down the floor, three against two.

Rules of Fast Breaking

- Look up and see the entire floor.
- Pass ahead to an open player.
- Run quickly down the court.
- Fill all lanes; wing players should stay wide.
- Make easy plays.
- Receivers should show target hands.

TWO-ON-ONE
Players shouldn't overpass on a fast break

The fast break should be the first option in any offense. Whether a player is by himself or with a few teammates, trying to score quickly and easily becomes an offensive weapon. The fast break allows teams to control the tempo of the game and creates easy scoring opportunities. A fast break can occur after a steal, rebound, made shot, or blocked shot.

Another important advantage of a fast break is that it gives everyone an opportunity to score. The more a player hustles and runs down court, the more opportunities he gets to make a few quick baskets. Make sure players don't get too happy and start "cherry picking." This occurs when a player runs down court every time the shot is up or doesn't run back on defense and waits down at the other end for a quick, easy shot.

Players must remember to rebound. When players run a two-on-one fast break, the ball should never be dribbled up

Two-on-one Half Court

- This is a great drill for warming up.

- Players start on the baseline and weave to half court. The player with the ball when reaching half court places it on the floor in the middle circle.

- He then runs back into the key area to play defense. One of the other two players picks up the ball.

- The player with the ball dribbles to a side, while the other player goes to the opposite side. A two-on-one break is formed.

Two-on-one

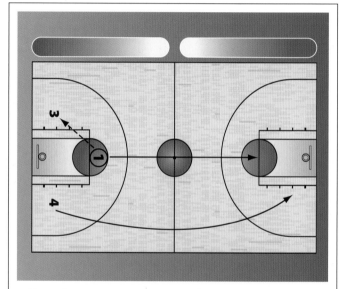

- Here, player 1 passes to either player 3 or 4.

- Player 1 then turns and sprints to the opposite foul line to play defense.

- Players 3 and 4 go down the floor looking to score on the defender.

the middle of the court. This allows the one defensive player to come back to play both. Players should pick a side and spread the floor to make it tough for the defensive player. The player with the ball should attack the basket after crossing the foul line plane area. If the defense doesn't guard the dribbler, the dribbler should continue going toward the basket for a layup. The opposite offensive player should run to block. If the defensive player commits to the dribbler, the dribbler then passes to teammates for an easy layup from the block area.

Make sure players do not overpass to each other. Overpassing gives the defense a chance to recover. Remind players to limit passes and to try to score quickly when doing two-on-one drills.

Two-on-one Drill

- Players line up on the baseline in three lines with the ball in the middle. The middle player walks out to the foul line and faces the baseline, while the others start at the block facing down court.

- The middle player passes the ball to either player

on the block. The receiver dribbles down court. The defensive player who threw the ball sprints to the three-point line and back pedals to the middle of the key.

- A two-on-one fast break takes place. The player who didn't receive the ball runs down to the opposite block.

Rules for a Two-on-one Fast Break

- Players must stay wide running in lanes.

- The ball should never be dribbled up the middle on a two-on-one break.

- Players should run toward the basket after crossing the foul line plane.

- The player with the ball should never pick up the ball only to pass.

- If the defense doesn't commit, the ball should be taken in for a layup.

ELEVEN-MAN FAST BREAK
This drill teaches multiple skills

The eleven-man fast break drill is among the most popular drills done in practice. It's a great full-court drill that emphasizes three-on-two, rebounding, outlet passes, transition, and conditioning. A minimum of eleven players is needed to do the drill.

The drill starts with two defensive players in the key area on both sides of the court in tandem formation. There are four lines on the sideline: Two lines on one side of half court

across from each other, two lines on the other side of half court. These lines are the outlet lines. The ball starts in the middle. Players play three-on-two when a shot is taken. All players on court can go after the ball. If the offense gets the ball, it can shoot again. If the defense gets the ball, it then outlets the ball to the sideline. This player then dribbles to the middle. The outlet pass player runs behind the dribbler to fill a lane down the other side of the court. The opposite

Tips for Eleven-man Fast Break

- Make sure all spots are filled on the defensive and outlet positions.

- If the ball is stolen quickly, push ball up. No outlet is needed here.

- If a player makes a basket, anyone can grab the ball out of the net and stay in the drill. The ball is alive for anyone to grab.

- Make sure all players talk during the drill.

Eleven Man

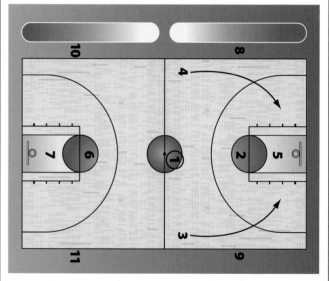

- The "1," "2," and "3" go down the floor against two defenders ("4" and "5").

- The two defenders rebound the ball and outlet it to "8" or "9." Then they come down the floor three on two.

- This drill is continuous. Make sure all spots are filled.

KNACK COACHING YOUTH BASKETBALL

152

sideline runs in his lane to fill out the three-on-two fast break. This process repeats itself down the other end. If the shot is made, all players can try to rebound the ball out of the net and get the ball to outlet to stay on court. All remaining players fill in on the sideline or defensive spots.

If a player makes a steal, that player is automatically on offense down the other end along with the two outlet players. They now just fill in lanes.

YELLOW ● LIGHT

This drill should be done with advanced players only after the transition defense has been taught. Offensive players will get easy layups in this drill. The two defenders must be talking in order for the defense to work. Players also need to learn how to space and need to know which lanes to run in.

Offensive Rebounding

- Eleven-man fast break teaches offensive rebounding. The ball is continuously alive throughout the drill. All players must go after the ball to stay in the drill. Players who are aggressive will get many turns during this drill.

- Players can work on making outlet passes and getting down on the fast break.

- This drill also allows for contact because all players go in for rebounds and try to stay in the drill.

Multiple Skills

- Eleven-man fast break teaches all types of skills: Rebounding, scoring, dribbling, passing, filling lanes, and defending.

- It allows players to have quick scoring opportunities and to spot up and shoot.

- From a defensive standpoint, it's a great drill for working on transition defense.

- Communication is key. Players must yell "Outlet," "Ball," and "Rebound" at all times.

- It also allows for many passing opportunities for players cutting to the basket.

CALLING PLAYS

Use visual and verbal cues to let your team know which plays to run

Coaches, assistant coaches, and players will call plays throughout the game. Plays and defensive sets will change during the game. When naming plays, be sure to keep the names simple. Use basic names, such as those of college teams, colors, or numbers. Using silly names causes players to laugh and not take the plays seriously.

In practice have your point guard call plays every time you run offensive sets. Different plays will be called for different situations. For example, when a ball goes out of bounds and is taken out under your basket, an out-of-bounds play is called. When a team is pressing you, you will call your press-breaker play. Use only one play per situation. Younger players forget; do not make plays complicated.

Before the game tell players which plays they will run. As your point guard brings the ball down, shout out the play and have the point guard repeat it. Plays can also be signals

Coach Calling Plays

- Before the game and during the game, timeouts, and halftime, players are consistently being reminded of which plays to run.

- As a coach, you must make sure these players know how to run the plays. It is useless to call out a play if players do not run it. Proper preparation must take place during practice.

- Don't be afraid to run the same play throughout the game, particularly if the play is working.

Player Calling Plays

- Make your point guard responsible for calling out the plays. Whether hand signals or verbal cues are used, players on court need to be aware of which play to run.

- As a coach, you will call out the play first, and then your point guard will repeat it.

- A good time for players to talk about running something new or to press is during a foul shot. Players are encouraged to gather around the player shooting and briefly discuss what will happen next.

so the other team doesn't know what you're running. For example, holding up a fist, waiving a hand, or holding up one or two fingers will signal a play. It's best to have both verbal and visual cues for your players so you can make sure your players get the message. There's nothing worse than having four players who are running the play and one person who has no idea what's happening. Sometimes the crowd is noisy, and your players can't hear you. And at other times your players have their backs to you. Have both types of cues ready or have players remind each other.

Slapping Ball

- The player who takes the ball out of bounds will receive it from the referee.

- At this time the player will hold the ball over her head and slap it. This sound and motion will signal the other players to run the play.

- As the ball goes out of bounds, call out which out-of-bounds play to run so your players can quickly get into the right spots.

- The player taking the ball out should shout out the play as well.

Tips on Running Plays

- Verbal cues: Cues should be called out loudly so everyone hears.

- Nonverbal cues: Cues need to be recognized by players.

- If the gym is too noisy, coaches can hold up signs to cue plays.

- Remind players to repeat plays going down court.

- Repeat plays, especially if the plays are working.

SPECIAL SITUATIONS

JT-OF-BOUNDS PLAYS

Make sure you get the type of shot you want

Out-of-bounds plays are run when the ball is knocked out by the opposing team, and it's your team's ball under your basket. You should have one or two set plays for this situation. The player taking the ball out of bounds usually is your "3" player, best passer, or player with the most sense. This player will slap the ball to indicate the other player to run the play. Remind the player taking the ball out of bounds not to stand behind the basket. He must take the ball out off to the side.

Your team will have five seconds to get the ball inbounds, and the player taking the ball out can't move, or else a traveling violation will be called.

Plays like this work so well because you have the opportunity to practice them ahead of time. You need to make sure your players execute. Players must set solid screens, rub off screens shoulder to shoulder, and cut quickly to the open spots or basket. Run plays for the right people. Make sure

Inbound-zone

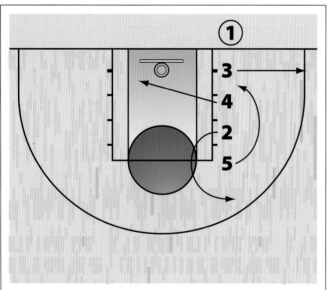

Box Inbounds

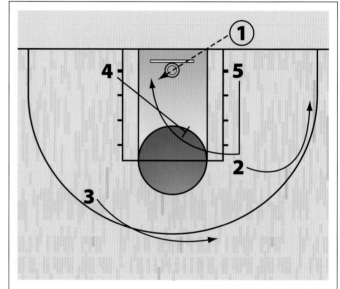

- This play is designed for players ages six to nine. It can be run against man-to-man defense but works better against zone.

- On the slap of the ball, the "3" cuts hard to the corner while calling for the ball. The "4" positions himself inside the middle defender while the "2" circles up top to be the safety, and "5" cuts to the open area.

- This inbounds play is designed for players ages ten to twelve.

- It is run mostly against man-to-man defense.

- Make sure that screens are set and that players wait for screens.

- On the slap of the ball, "5" upscreens for "2," who goes to the corner. The "4" diagonal screens for "5," who goes to the opposite block. The "3" comes up top to be the safety.

players know their roles. Out-of-bounds plays are used to get a quick shot off or to get the ball inbounds to run an offense. Set screens so your best player is in position to shoot. Multiple screens can be set simultaneously to get players open.

Timing is critical in order to run plays effectively. Players should set up the defense before coming off a screen by jabbing one way first and then going the opposite way toward the screen. Your plays should always have a purpose; don't let yourself or your players lose sight of this purpose. Do you want a layup out of the inbounds? Do you want a three-point shot? Or do you just want to get the ball in? Whatever the play is, it must be run correctly and practiced numerous times. It's also good to have an inbounds play that can be used against both man and zone.

Advanced Inbounds

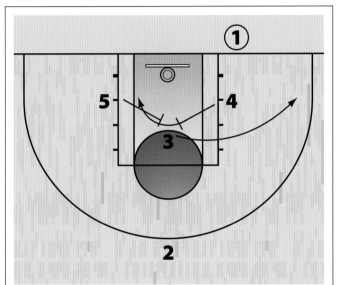

- This play is to be used against a man-to-man defense.

- It is ideal for players ages thirteen to fourteen.

- On the slap of the ball, "4" screens for "3," who goes out to the corner. The "5" screens for "4," who goes to the opposite block, and "5" opens to the ball.

Tips on Taking the Ball out of Bounds

- Players can't move after the ref gives them the ball.

- Players should not stand under the basket.

- Players slap the ball or call out "Go" for the play to start.

- The player must throw the ball inbounds within five seconds.

- After he passes the ball in, the player must also go inbounds.

ZONE OFFENSES

These formations attack areas, not players

A zone offense is similar to a man offense with a few adjustments. In a man offense, you attack players, but in a zone offense, you attack areas. Cuts aren't as important as spacing and positioning. Ball movement is essential in throwing off the defense. Quick, sharp passes along with skip passes force the defense to move out of position. As the ball moves, the players need to slide into "dead spots" in the zone. "Dead spots," or gaps, are areas that aren't covered by the defense.

Those spots provide open lanes for the offense.

Youth basketball plays, in particular zone offenses, are easy to teach, and players can quickly learn their positions on the court. These zone plays have to be easy enough for athletes to remember but still be effective. Zone plays require few screens, if any, so zone offenses are easy for youth players to learn.

Place guards in three spots on court—at point and two

Zone Offense

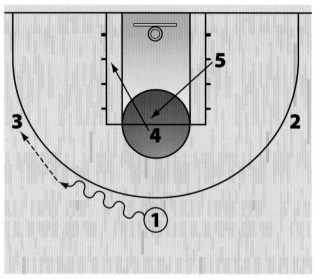

Zone Offense (Continued)

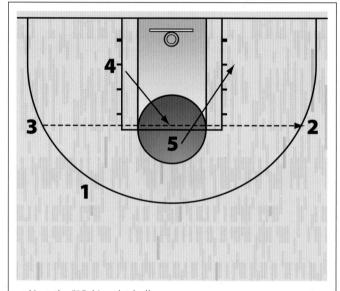

- This zone offense can be used for players six to nine years of age.

- A basic zone offense is the post interchanging from the high post to the low post based on which side the ball is on.

- The "1" passes the ball to the "3." On the pass, the player at the foul line will dive to the block, and the opposite post player will come high to the foul line area.

- Next the "3" skips the ball to "2." The "5" will dive to the block, and "4" will come high.

wings. Your forwards can be interchangeable. You can have the forwards at each box, or you can have a forward/center run in a triangle formation. This player goes from high post to either box. Zone offenses allow players to learn spacing and positions.

At the youth age, zone offenses don't require much movement. Zone offenses have positives and negatives. One positive of a zone offense is that younger players more easily can understand where to stand on the court. Zone offenses create spacing and prevent players from surrounding the ball. One negative of playing zone at the youth level is that players tend to stand around and not cut, or they think they aren't allowed to move and so just stand and watch.

Advanced Zone Offense

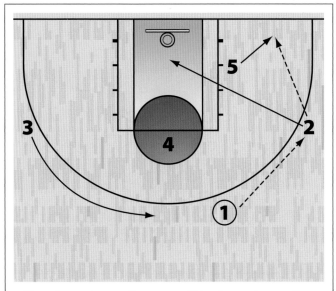

- The advanced zone offensive has a player pop out to the short corner from the post area.

- This play is diagrammed to have the wings cutting through the lane and all players constantly moving.

- This advanced zone offense should be run only with players thirteen years old and older.

- The "1" passes to "2," and "5" steps to the short corner area. The "2" passes to "5" and then cuts through the lane looking for the ball initially.

Advanced Zone Offense (Continued)

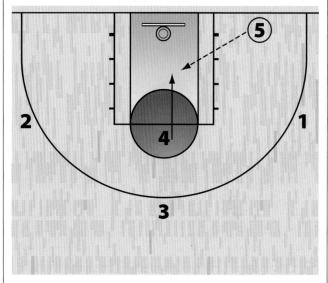

- Next the "3" comes up to the top. After "2" cuts, "4" cuts to the middle of the lane looking for a pass from "5."

- The pattern continues if "5" doesn't pass to "2" or "4."

MAN-TO-MAN OFFENSES

Developing offenses for the team is the most visible part of a coach's job

An offense is a series of cuts, passes, and screens that is designed to create particular shots for certain players. You need an offense to provide organization and objectives so players have a clear idea of what they are trying to accomplish. You can run your offense in two ways: By being a "system" coach or a "nonsystem" coach. A system coach runs the same offense year after year. A nonsystem coach changes plays each year based on his players. This type of coach constructs an offense specifically for the players on the team. A coach should do a little of both at this youth level. Be consistent in running specific plays but feel free to explore and implement new ones. Remember not to overdo it with

Motion Offense

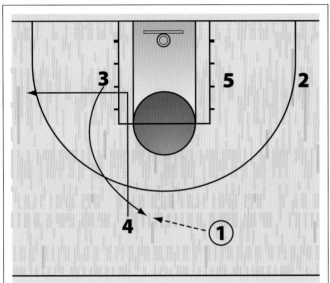

- The motion offense can be used for players six to twelve years of age.

- Modify this offense for beginners by having players pass and screen away. The guards will screen for each other, and the forwards will screen for each other.

- To start the offense, "4" will screen down on "3," who comes up to the elbow. The "4" will pop to the baseline wing.

Motion Offense (Continued)

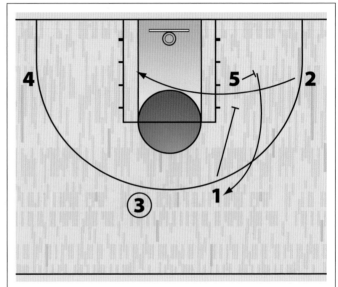

- Meanwhile, as "3" catches the ball, "5" will screen for "2," who comes to the ball-side block.

- As soon as "2" comes off the screen, "1" will screen down for "5," who comes to the elbow. The "1" will pop to the baseline wing.

many plays, especially with players younger than the seventh grade.

After the ball goes up and the game starts, there is little you can do to make decisions for your players. Be sure to have your players prepared in practice so they feel more comfortable in game situations. Several factors must be taught when implementing an offense: Spacing, angles, timing, role definitions, and objectives. More advanced players will develop these factors as they reach high school. Most importantly, teaching proper spacing, some basic cuts, and screens will

at least allow youth players to get in somewhat of an offense set. Your players have to know what they are expected to do within the offense and what their abilities and talent can bring to the team.

Many youth teams have that first-shot mentally, which is fine because younger players don't yet have the concept of passing down. Making a basket at the beginner level is a huge deal for kids. Let them shoot as much as they can.

Offense with Four High

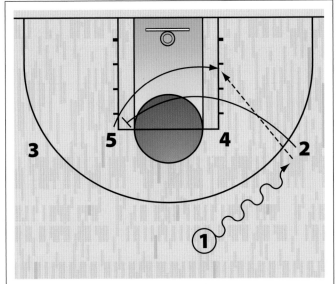

- A four-high formation pulls both posts up to the elbow area.

- Advantages of the four high include spacing and back-down cuts along with having on-t-e ball screens.

- The "1" will dribble at "2," who goes to the backdoor initially.

Offense with Four High (Continued)

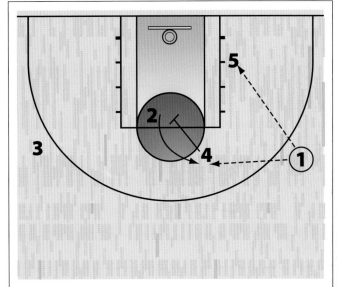

- The "2" does not receive the ball, so he will upscreen for "5."

- The "1" looks for "5" on the block.

- Meanwhile, "4" screens for "2."

SIDELINE PLAYS

It's better to have a few good plays than to overload your team with too many

Set plays are strategically planned and choreographed sequences of movements to get open shots and to score points. These plays are designed to go through one time with the hope of scoring. Set plays are quick hitters to score points at a certain point during the game. They should not be your entire offensive system. You should use set plays, such as a

sideline play, throughout the game. Times to use set plays include after timeouts, at the beginning of games, at the end of games, and when you really need a basket.

Picking the right set play can be exciting, especially when the play is executed to perfection. Different formations can be used to set up a sideline play. Many coaches like the

Basic Sideline

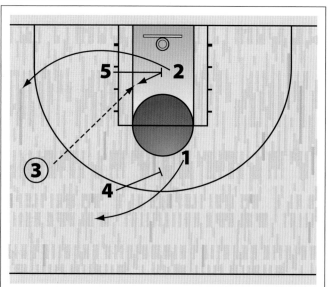

Box Sideline Inbounds

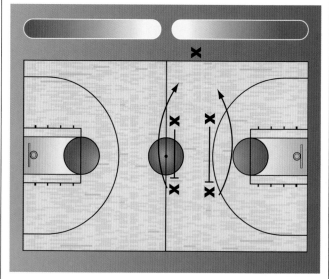

- This basic sideline play requires two basic screens.

- Player pops to corner after getting a screen from the center. Center posts, and forward screens for guard coming to ball.

- On the slap of the ball, "5" screens in the middle of the lane for "2," who goes to the baseline out to the corner.

- The "4" screens across for "1." And "5" screens and comes back to the ball. The "3" passes directly to "5."

- Players set up in a box formation at the top of the key to half court.

- On the slap of the ball, the players screen across.

- Players come to the ball. This box formation is basic to get the ball inbounds.

- After the two players screen, they can roll.

stack-and-box formation. Especially at the youth level, kids can remember where to go.

Advanced Sidelines

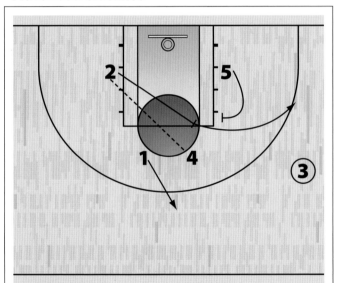

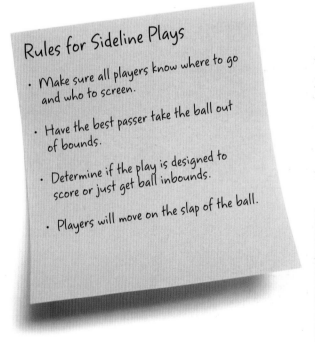

Rules for Sideline Plays

- Make sure all players know where to go and who to screen.

- Have the best passer take the ball out of bounds.

- Determine if the play is designed to score or just get ball inbounds.

- Players will move on the slap of the ball.

- On the slap of the ball, "1" will come out past the top of the key.

- The "2" will back pass for "4," who goes to the front of the rim.

- The "5" turns and screens for "2," who cuts to the baseline area.

PRESS BREAKER

Although many leagues limit pressing, have your team prepared to break a press

When attacking a zone press, you want to attack with patience. Too often coaches try to rush because they do not want to get called for a ten-second violation, rushing plays right into what a press is trying to accomplish. Everybody thinks teams press to steal the ball. That is obviously one goal the defense is hoping for, but what the defense is really trying to do is take you out of your comfort zone, make you hurry so you rush a shot, cause a turnover, or force a timeout. The biggest key to beating a press is to relax and recognize what kind of press your opponent is running.

Pressing defenses include full court, three-quarter court, and half court. There are two main objectives of any press

Basic Press Breaker

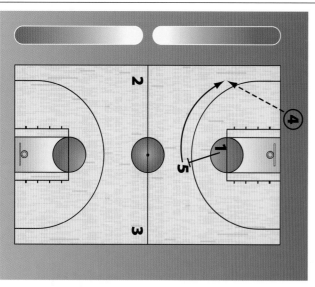

- You can use this press breaker against a man or a zone defense.

- The "1" upscreens for "5," who comes to the wing, and "1" stays in the middle of the floor.

- The "4" passes to "5," who looks for "1" in the middle of the floor.

Stack Press Breaker

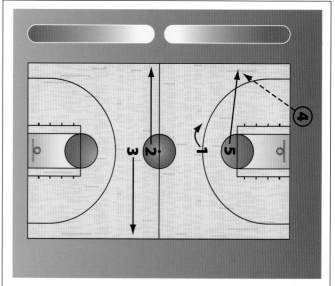

- On the slap of the ball, 5 cuts to the ballside wing. The "4" passes to "5" and steps inbounds.

- If "5" can't pass to "1" in the middle, "2" up the sideline, or "3" cross court, then he passes back to "4."

- The 4 takes a dribble to change sides of the floor. He passes to "3," while "1" cuts up the sideline, and "2" flashes to the middle of the floor.

- The "5" will fill the opposite wing.

breaker: To bring the ball across the ten-second line to get into your half-court offense and to score against the press. Three rules need to be followed when breaking the press:

1. Stay away from sidelines. Most pressing defenses want to position you where you can be double teamed or step out of bounds.

2. Do not throw the long pass unless your player has gotten ahead of his defender enough for a clear pass. This usually happens only against full-court man-to-man presses.

3. Pass the ball on the press. Try not to dribble that much against a press breaker. It's the slowest and least effective way of advancing the ball up the court. It's a method that invites traps and double teams. Passing is the way to go. There will be open players; it's your team's job to find them. Even if you have to pass backward, doing so can open up lanes and allow you to advance the ball in a quick, timely manner. Players should be spread out on the court to create options to break the press.

"1"-"5" Press Breakers

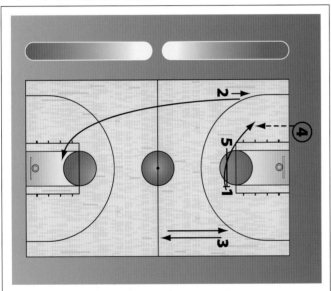

- This press breaker can be used against both man and zone.

- The "2" steps to the ball, then goes long. The "5" screens across for "1," who curls "5."

- The 3 breaks long and then comes back to the ball. The "4" can pass to the "2" long, the "1," or the "3."

Rules for Breaking a Press

- Spread the floor and cover all sections of the court. Positioning of your players is the most important part of being able to break a press.

- React to what the defense does.

- Get ball inbounds.

- Pass ball, don't dribble (dribbling should always be a last resort in press breaking).

LAST-SECOND SHOTS
Timing is critical to control the ball in these plays

Last-second shots can come at the end of quarters or at the end of the game. If you have the lead, and there are twenty seconds left in the quarter, you want to hold the ball for the last shot to increase your lead or to maintain your lead without allowing the opposing team a chance to score. Have players start to set up the play with ten seconds left and shoot the ball with five to six seconds remaining. This allows time for an offensive rebound and maybe a second shot but not enough time

for your opponent to get the ball and dribble down court. Do not wait until the buzzer to have your player shoot. This puts too much pressure on him to make the shot

One of the most important keys to being successful with last second plays is to create more than one scoring opportunity. By giving the ball handler more than one option on the play, easy scoring opportunities are created. Plus, the defense has a more difficult time defending the play and preventing a basket.

Half-court Last-second Shot

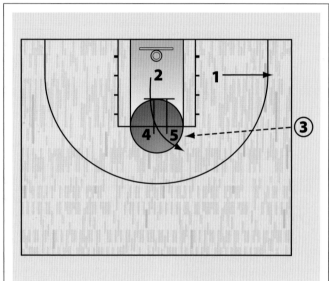

- Here "1" cuts to the same-side corner, calling for the ball.
- The "4" and "5" set a double screen for your best shooter.

Last-second Shot

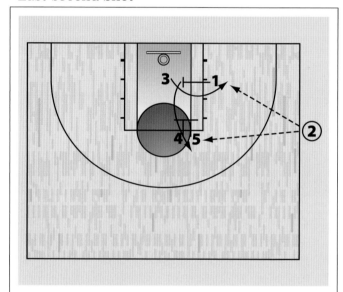

- The "1" screens across for "3." The "2"'s first look is "3."
- The "4" and "5" will set a double screen for "1" to come up for a shot at the foul line if you need a two-pointer or behind the three-point line if you need a three-pointer.

Use timeouts wisely. Call a timeout to go over the play your team will use. Make sure all players know where they will go and who will be the shooter. The last second play should be reviewed in practice; however, it must be reviewed again to refresh players' minds. After the timeout, when all players come onto court, you can see the defense's set up. Then can call another timeout and readjust to the defense's play. Most importantly, make sure your team is ready and on the same page to win the game.

Advanced Last-second Shot

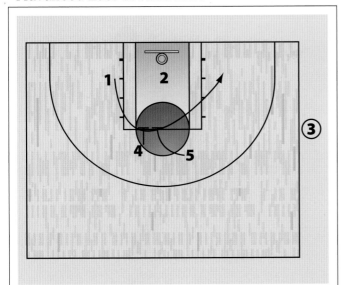

- On the slap of the ball, 1 comes off of "4" and "5"'s screens.

- The "1" doesn't get the ball but rather continues to the baseline.

Advanced Last-second Shot (Continued)

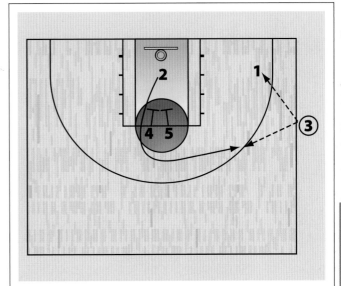

- Meanwhile, the "2" comes right after "1."

- The "4" and "5" set a second double screen for "2."

TEAM-BUILDING GAMES
Make every kid feel a part of the team

Drills need to be a part of every basketball practice. Drills are necessary to improve individual and team skills. Some drills are difficult, other drills are easy. Some players consider drills to be fun, whereas others consider drills to be hard and boring. Coaches must provide players with a combination of both fun and difficulty while incorporating necessary skills for improvement.

Different drills are necessary at different times. For example, preseason drills tend to be more intense and difficult. As the season progresses and your team is in season, a different set of drills may be used. Keep in mind that coaches must make the kids experience a fun and enjoyable season. Throwing in some team-building drills during the course of your season is a must.

As a coach, do not be concerned with what your players think of your drills. If there is a purpose for running a drill and

Name Tags

- Name tags are useful during the first few days of practice.

- Coaches should remember all players' names by the first week.

- Having name tags allows you to call out to players for certain drills, and you will be able to get their attention faster.

- Name tags should be put in front of the T-shirts and the names written in black marker.

- Name tags also help players on teams call out their teammates' names.

Mirror Dribbling

- The mirror dribbling drill works on keeping the head up, communicating with teammates, and conditioning. Change dribble moves throughout the drill.

- Form two lines of six players. Have three players on baseline and three at half court in a line facing the other line. First two players have a ball and dribble at each other, making the same move. Coach will determine the move. Players must stay close to each other when making the move and then speed dribble to the opposite line to give the ball to next two players to do same dribble move.

the drill is effective, then it should be run as often as needed. However, that doesn't mean that the coach can't try to make it fun and competitive by adding a twist.

One of the keys to building basketball team skills is to play fun games. Whether it's a simple game of tag, relay races, knockout, or half-court shots, make sure the atmosphere is light and enjoyable. This allows players to enjoy the competitive nature of the game and just have fun.

With parents' permission a good idea is to take players somewhere outside the game, whether it's going for pizza, going to a sports event, bowling, or having a barbecue. It doesn't really matter what you do. Just by getting players away from the game, you all can learn more about each other and grow together.

Partner Passing

- Partner passing develops team chemistry and allows players to get to know each other.

- Start by having players pick a partner. Partners stand across from each other and pass the ball to each other, calling out each other's names. Blow the whistle after a few times, and players should rotate to the right. Only one partner rotates.

- A different pass is now performed with a different partner, and names have to be called.

- This drill allows all players to pass to different teammates.

Foul Shots

- All players line up around the foul line like they would during a game. One player shoots a foul shot and then rotates so all players get a chance to shoot.

- Divide the players on the team in half. Players have to make that many shots (for example: Twelve players, six shots must be made).

- If the team doesn't reach its goal, it will have to run sprints based on the number of shots not made.

FUN GAMES: 6–9-YEAR-OLDS

Good coaches help players learn appropriate skills while having fun

Young basketball players are playing to have fun. Having fun is really all about the attitude of the coach and the attitude of the players. As coach, you must keep an upbeat attitude and keep the spirit of practice positive. This keeps practice moving and makes it less boring. And kids will enjoy each drill.

There are several benefits of making practice and drills fun. Make sure you incorporate the right kind of fun drills

and not silly, out-of-control drills that can get players hurt. Most basketball drills are boring and monotonous. Young players do not want to be yelled at by coaches for every mistake, and coaches don't want to always try to keep players on task. Allowing players to explore how to play will benefit everyone in the long run. As a coach, you will see your players be more enthusiastic. Attitudes will improve, and players will enjoy fitness activities and get in better

Candyland

- Dump a bunch of wrapped candies into the middle of the floor. Have players line up evenly on all four corners of the court.

- When music starts, one player from each of the four lines slides to middle, picks up a piece of candy, and does a defensive slide back

to line. Then the next player goes. After everyone goes, switch up the move to the middle. Players then have to dribble the ball, pick up candy, and dribble back.

- When music stops, team with the most candy wins and gets to have the rest of the candy in the middle.

Hoop Basketball

- Place two hula hoops of different colors in center of court with three balls in each. Divide team into two teams, giving each player on the teams a number. Players should sit on the sideline.

- Call out three numbers. Those six players run to their hula hoop, grab a ball, and

dribble to their basketball. Players stay at the basket and shoot until the shot is made. After basket is made, players dribble back to hula hoop, place ball in hoop, and run back and sit in line.

- Points are awarded by the number of players from the losing team left standing.

condition without even knowing it. Players will learn to love the game, and you will have more fun coaching it.

Drills that are fun but that at the same time incorporate valuable basketball skills are the most important. By having this combination you will see a big improvement in the skills of your players. Keep in mind that youth players' attention spans are short, so don't spend too much time on one drill. The drill becomes boring, or players become unfocused.

Stoplight

- It's hard for younger kids to develop control over their bodies. Playing "Stop and Go" games help them practice control.

- Players start on baseline dribbling ball. Coach has back to players on opposite baseline. Coach yells "green light" and players dribble up court. Coach turns and yells "red light" and players must stop and pick up the ball. If player continues to dribble, drops ball, or doesn't stop, they are out. Play continues until first player reaches baseline.

- Make players dribble with certain hands.

Cat-and-mouse

- All players with balls line up on the baseline. Two players without a ball in the middle of the court are the cats. When the two players yell, "Meow," this signals the other players to run to get safely to the opposite side.

- If the cat tags the mouse (players dribbling), then that player becomes a cat. The more cats who tag the mice, the more players are in the middle. Players must dribble the ball and cannot step out of the court area.

- Coach signals cats to meow so the drill is done in a controlled manner.

FUN GAMES: 10–12-YEAR-OLDS

Drills that involve winning and losing typically involve practicing pressure shots

As players mature and have a few years of basketball under their belts, games still need to be incorporated. Coaches must continue their upbeat attitude and provide players with drills that are fun and productive. All players are competitors and want to win. Players practice hard because they want to win and improve their own level of play. Coaches can make the drills competitive in practice to bring out the best in everyone.

Coaches should make competitive drills that involve the team. You can divide the team into two so players compete against the clock. Having players reach a certain number of shots or getting a drill done in a certain amount of time

Knockout

- Knockout is the most popular game played. Players line up behind each other at the foul line.

- The first two players have balls. The first player shoots ball from the foul line. If players make the shot, they get the rebound and give the ball to the next player. If the first player misses, he must rebound and try to make the shot before the player behind him makes his shot. If the other player makes the shot first, that player is out.

- Knockout can be played with all age groups and can be played from the three-point line.

Advanced Hoop Basketball

- Advanced hoop basketball is set up the same way as regular hoop basketball except shots are taken from different spots.

- When numbers are called, the coaches tell the players what to do. For example, the first shot must be a three-pointer, then all other shots can be layups.

- Another variation is to have players dribble to the opposite end of the court, touch the baseline, and dribble down the court to the basket to shoot.

makes players work hard to accomplish the goals. The winning team can make the losing team do sprints, push-ups, or something fun. Or the winning team can get a water break first. Changing up the penalty for losing allows players to be creative and enjoy the anticipation.

A player's input is also important. Coaches should be aware when a drill isn't fun or is unproductive. You will be able to tell when a drill is fun. Players will jump around and laugh, cheer, and smile. They won't mind doing a sprint or a push-up if they lose, and they will ask to play the game again. On the flip side, when the drill becomes too competitive and players are getting frustrated, then it's time to revise the drill or completely stop it. When this happens, players' frustration is taken out on their teammates. This defeats the purpose of playing fun games. Incorporate fun games toward the end of practice or set aside a certain day of practice that will be used for fun drills.

Dribble Tag

- In dribble tag all players are scattered around the court dribbling a ball, each player for herself. When the whistle blows, players try to knock balls out of other players' hands while dribbling their own ball.

- Dribble tag is played with basketball rules, which means no walking or double dribbling.

- If a ball is knocked out, then the player is out. As the game goes on, shorten the boundaries to make it harder for players. A boundary would be inside the three-point line and then inside the foul line.

Hot Shot

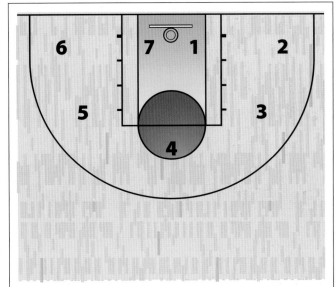

- Hot shot is a popular summer camp game but can be used in practices and can be modified.

- Players will shoot from seven different spots on the court in one minute. Each shot is worth one point.

- There are seven hot shot spots. Spots 1 and 7 are layups; the rest are jump shots.

- This is a great drill to do at the end of practice or during camp. Time kids for one minute, with each shot worth four points. The kids must follow the shots in order.

173

FUN GAMES: 13–14-YEAR-OLDS
Players are never too old to have fun

Players who are thirteen or fourteen have developed a true sense of how to play the game and have seen their share of coaches, whether it's a middle school basketball team, CYO, travel, or AAU. Players at this point know which coaches they like and which coaches have made their basketball experience enjoyable. Each player develops at a different rate, and coaches develop as well. Most importantly, coaches need to be consistent in teaching players the correct drills and

making sure they aren't letting players just play but rather are teaching the game to these players at this age level. Effective coaches use game play to help players understand why certain events happen in games. Coaches can still incorporate fun drills, but now these drills are for teaching shot selection and passing to teammates. For example, a scrimmage game can be played by changing two rules. No dribbling: The ball must be advanced with a pass, and no blocking or stealing

Two in a Row

- A more advanced way of doing team relays is making two shots in a row. Instead of the whole team shooting for a total of ten shots made from a spot, the team is required to make two shots in a row in order to move to the next spot.

- Start the team with power layups. There are two balls in each line. When two shots are made in a row, all players move to the next spot, which will be in the corner. After two shots are made, players move to wing, foul line, wing, and then opposite corner.

Taps

- Two players line up on the box opposite each other; two other players start opposite each other at the elbow.

- Players at elbow shoot; if they make it, they get one point. If shot is missed, other two players try to tap in ball. Players' feet must leave the

ground, and only two taps are allowed. If ball is tapped in, players are awarded two points, and they now switch with players at elbow. Game is played to 21 with a three-point shot having to be made to end game. If ball is not tapped in successfully, then players do not switch. Play continues.

the ball from an offensive player. A defender may contest the offensive player but can't steal or block. This teaches players to move without the ball and to pass to each other.

Coaches should always keep in mind that basketball is meant to be fun, although at times it seems to get pretty competitive, especially as the level of play improves. You want this to be a memorable experience for players, and you want them to continue playing.

Four-on-four Full

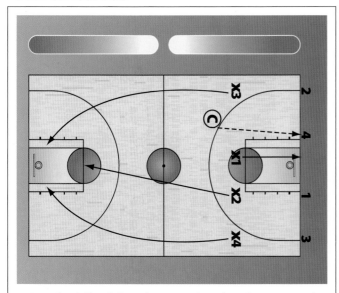

- Start the drill with four players across the baseline and four across the foul line.

- The coach throws the ball to one of the baseline players. The player in front of the player who catches the ball has to touch the baseline.

- The other players sprint the floor and form a triangle.

- The four offensive players come down the floor four on three until the other player catches up.

Pop Up

- Pop up is a one-on-one game. Have players lie on their stomachs on the sideline.

- Give them all a number. Call out two numbers. When a player's number is called, she gets up off the ground and runs after the ball. Whoever reaches the ball first is on offense, the other on defense. These two players play one on one until a basket is scored.

- The coach should bounce the ball high into the air so the two players can fight for possession.

175

RELAY RACES

Exercises can be fun and develop team chemistry

Good team chemistry is important for the success of all team sports, particularly in basketball. Basketball involves quick passes and communication. Chemistry can be improved by doing simple team-building drills that allow players to succeed and be encouraged by teammates.

One of the favorite and easiest ways to develop team building is through relay races. Relay races are so useful because they are easy, fun, and competitive. Relay races can be used in dribble lines, shooting lines, and conditioning lines. Coaches must try to keep relay lines as even as possible so the drill is competitive. Make sure rules are clear and that every player understands what to do. Younger players can start off with dribble relay races. Divide your team into three lines of four in each or two lines of six, depending on the number of players you have.

Change the drill after players go four times. Maybe start

Dribble Races

- Dribble relay races are great for dribbling at game speed.

- Be sure to put players in equal lines to keep it fair.

- Dribbling races are great for camps and clinics.

- Different dribbles should be performed. It's a great way to force kids to use their left hand and to make them look up to see where they dribble to and from.

Shooting Relays

- Shooting relays can be done from any spot on court, and the number of shots made will be determined by the coach.

- Here are examples of shooting relays: Number of layups made, number of shots made, number of shots made in a minute.

- Players love competing, and shooting relays make them enthusiastic.

- Shooting relays develop team chemistry and encourage players to cheer.

with right hand up and back, next time left up and left back. Relay races can be done without the ball as useful conditioning drills. Players can sprint to the end and back, they can do a defensive slide up and back, and maybe they can do a grapevine run. Players can also do different exercises when they get to the end line. Push-ups, sit-ups or jumping jacks can be incorporated. Even if players do a dribbling drill, they can put the ball down and do a push-up or a sit-up and dribble back.

Shooting relay races can be done by shooting layups or jump shots from certain spots on the floor. Have players try to make ten shots as a team or maybe two shots in a row. Then they can advance to the next spot. Many variations of shooting relay races can be done.

Conditioning Relays

- Conditioning relays are set up the same way as dribble relays, except no ball is used.

- They are a great way to start up a practice by warming kids up with various running techniques.

- Running techniques, such as grapevine, butt kicks, high knees, and defensive slides, should be used.

- Adding push-ups and sit-ups to the conditioning part will also build players' strengths. This allow players to get into basketball shape.

Skill Free-for-all

- Skill free-for-all is a rating skill game that consists of five skills: Crab walk, line sprints, hot shot, X-out, and wall pass. All skills are timed for thirty seconds.

- Each player performs one skill at a time; you can put two or three players at a basket.

- Record each player's score.

ONE-ON-ONE GAMES

Players' offensive skills will improve by playing one-on-one; match players up accordingly

One-on-one games provide players a chance to work on moves to score. Players can polish their moves, test new moves, and improve their individual game. One-on-one games can be played full court, half court, with chairs, and when conditioning one-on-one.

One-on-one rules should be set before games are played.

If you have five players per basket and it's continuous, the coaches must decide if it's winners or losers out. One-on-one games are scored with each basket worth one point. Usually the game ends when a player scores eleven points. Players must call their own fouls. If they are fouled, then they simply recheck the ball. Coaches should limit the number of dribbles.

Close Out

- One-on-one close out works on both defensive and offensive skill work.

- Setup: Five players are at a basket. One player starts at the foul line, the rest line up under the basket.

- First player slowly rolls ball out to foul line player. The

receiver can then shoot, drive to basket, and continue to play one-on-one. If the defense gets ball, it becomes the offense. The first offensive player goes to the end of the line. Next player in line rolls ball out. This continues. If the offensive player scores, he stays on offense.

Slide One-on-one

- Slide one-on-one works when defense slides are used before one-on-one is played.

- Two players face each other in the key area. Both players slide to the sideline and then slide back to the key area.

- The player closest to the foul line back pedals up the lane line to the elbow and receives the ball from the coach. At this time a one-on-one game takes place.

- Adding slides before the players play allows one-on-one to be more game like.

This will force players to try to score and not dribble around, as younger players tend to do. Players must always bring the ball back to a clearing point after a defensive rebound is made. If a steal or block shot happens, players can go right up with the shot and not take it back. More advanced players can use the three-point line; however, in this drill a basket is worth two points because all other baskets are worth one point. Incorporating the three-point line as a scoring threat forces the defense to play tighter up-close defense.

To start a game of one-on-one, players will check ball.

"Checking ball" simply means the defense bounce passes the ball to the offensive players, which begins the game. Coaches make sure the "check" is a bounce pass and not a forceful chest pass. Checking is a standard way to start play.

Triangle One-on-one

- Here both players start opposite each other at the box. One player has the ball. This player slowly rolls it to the foul line.

- At this time the opposite player slides to the box and then slides up to the foul line to play defense.

- This drill works on defense quickly closing out and getting up to the player.

- Offensively the player should react quickly to take advantage of his early start.

Fade One-on-one

- Fade one-on-one starts with both players opposite each other on the baseline, one lane line apart.

- The player with the ball dribbles up to the elbow. He then throws the ball to the other player and fades back to the wing area. The opposite player runs to the

mid-foul line and throws the ball to the player who faded.

- At this time the player who threw the ball quickly runs out to play defense. The one-on-one game now starts.

GOALS

Assess players for mental as well as physical qualities

What are your immediate goals when starting tryouts? You want to find the best mix of players. You might need certain positions filled because of graduation. Each tryout will be different, depending on what type of team you are coaching. Players ages six to nine all make the team, so tryouts won't be held at this level. Players ages ten to twelve will try out for CYO, recreation, and AAU teams, and players will try out for school teams. These programs might have two teams at each grade level or combine fifth- and sixth-graders and seventh- and eighth-graders.

Tryouts should last no more than three sessions. Allow for at least an hour to find the best fit for your team. When evaluating players, have someone help you. This person should not be a parent but maybe an assistant coach or a friend with knowledge of the game.

So how does a player impress you with her skills? You

Tryout Flyer

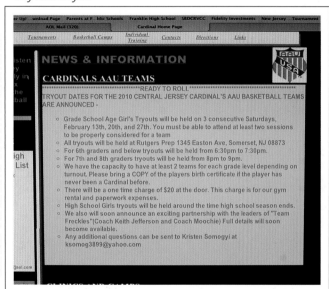

- A tryout flyer can be sent out through e-mail or the postal service and given out at basketball games.

- The flyer should state time, location, and date of tryouts.

- Give contact information, such as a cell phone number

- or e-mail address, for any questions regarding tryouts.

- Remind players to wear proper basketball clothes.

- State if there is a cost to try out and if kids need to bring any necessary information with them, such as a birth certificate.

Calendar

- Have a calendar with all practices and games printed on each date. Figure that your season will last just over three months, so take out three months of the year. A full twelve-month calendar is not necessary.

- Highlight game times and any necessary events, such as a fundraiser or a pizza party.

- If you have a Web site, be sure to post the calendar so parents can refer to it.

should look for players with solid fundamentals: Kids who play tough defense, hustle after loose balls, and play aggressively, kids who box out, rebound, and play defense. Even if a kid misses all his shots, you will be able to see that he knows how to do a layup or shoot a jump shot the proper way.

Players who are first in line, who pay attention, and who are first to arrive at the gym will catch your eye. At the youth level, all players have potential to improve. Take that into consideration.

During tryouts have players participate in both offensive and defensive drills. Keep the lines moving. Incorporate one-on-one drills and eventually move to scrimmaging. Give all players the opportunity to succeed. During the last tryouts, start to separate the stronger and weaker players so you can get a final roster.

Looking for a Mix

- Tryouts can be stressful on coaches. Making sure that you pick the correct players and cutting players can take their toll.

- Remind players that coaches like team players. Coaches don't like players who do too much and are too fancy. Keep it basic and avoid turnovers.

- Players should understand that there will always be a few players at tryouts who are better players and will make the team but that certain players can also play an important part as "role players."

Tips for Coaches During Tryouts

- Be positive.

- Demonstrate drills.

- Encourage players throughout tryouts.

- Give feedback to players at end of practice.

HOW MANY TO KEEP ON A TEAM?

Different levels and different teams allow ten to fifteen players per team

Recreation departments require players to register for league play, and then players are placed on a team. All players make a team. Typically beginner players join a recreation program. The number of players varies from ten to fifteen players. These recreation leagues play once a week on Saturday mornings, with a practice during the week. Players are given a T-shirt as a uniform top with a number on the back. Everyone plays equally. Basic fundamentals are taught at this level.

The next level of play is travel, CYO, school team, and AAU. Players can be on a couple of teams during the winter season. CYO and travel usually start when players are ten years of age or in fourth grade. Players are asked to try out. A

Recreation/Youth Players

- At this level all players will be put on a team.

- Players will pay a small fee to participate in the league. A T-shirt is given to be worn during game play.

- Coaches are usually volunteers or parents of players.

- Referees during the games don't make a lot of the regular calls. Instead they try to teach the players how to play and allow many violations to go uncalled.

CYO/Travel Players

- CYO and travel teams participate in league play. Games are typically on the weekend, with practice once or twice a week.

- Full uniforms are issued for players to wear.

- Typical game season lasts three months, with about twenty games. Playoffs take place at the end of the season.

- Travel teams in particular play in different tournaments throughout the year in addition to league play.

typical team consists of twelve players. Depending on the team, the roster can go up to fifteen. As a coach, don't feel bad about cutting players. It's your job to pick your team and move forward. Players always have recreational leagues to fall back on.

School teams and AAU require a separate category of tryouts. Although players can play both school and travel, not all players are guaranteed playing time at this level. Trying out for these teams can be tough on players. Some middle school teams have over sixty boys trying out for twelve spots.

AAU is typically the same, except there are a lot more AAU teams to try out for.

School teams sometimes include sixth-graders and allow them to try out. A school team can consist of sixth-, seventh-, and eighth-graders or just seventh- and eighth-graders. There are also B teams at this level for younger grades. AAU teams are picked during the spring months and can continue into the summer. AAU rules require players to be of appropriate age or grade level. Teams are designated by their age group, for example, U10s, U11s, and so forth.

Advanced Players

- At this level players will be cut from teams. This prepares them for later on when they try out for their high school teams.

- Players who continue to play seventh- and eighth-grade travel or CYO and don't try out for a school team or AAU will continue with the same tryout patterns.

- School teams and AAU teams tend to have the more advanced players who are looking for top competition.

Levels of Competition

- Recreation league
- CYO league
- Travel league
- AAU

RATING SYSTEM
Evaluate players on a scale from 1 to 5

One of the most exciting and stressful parts of a young player's life can be trying out for an athletic team when he has to show a coach he deserves to be on a team. Some players are extremely confident in their abilities, and some players have a lot of self-doubt or no confidence in themselves. As a coach, you have to look past what might be obvious on the court and see if a player's personality or lack of confidence is keeping the player's real talent from being shown.

When holding a tryout, a rating system should be in place to evaluate each player. Players who are trying out should wear a number on their backs so the evaluators can identify them. Have two evaluators who aren't court coaches pick the team. Ultimately you will have the final say, but having other people's input is important.

When evaluating players, look at the most obvious things first: Attitude and athleticism. Players who are enthusiastic

Rating System

CARDINAL TRYOUT EVALUATION FORM

Evaluator Name _____ Date _____ Age Group _____

(THE HIGHER THE NUMBER THE BETTER THE SCORE)

	BASKETBALL SKILLS						PHYSICAL STRENGTHS					MISCELLANEOUS				
PLAYER #	JUMP SHOOTING	LAYUPS	DRIBBLING	PASSING	DEFENSE	OVERALL SKILLS	HEIGHT	SPEED	QUICKNESS	STRENGTH		MENTAL POISE	DRIVE HUSTLE		TOTAL	BEST POSITION
SCALE	1 - 10	1 - 10	1 - 10	1 - 10	1 - 10	1 - 10	1 - 15	1 - 15	1 - 10	1 - 10		1 - 10	1 - 10			1 - 5

Posting Cuts

- The rating system is broken down into offense and defense.

- Offensive skills include dribbling, shooting, passing, and court awareness.

- These skills can then be broken down into more specifics, such as dribbling

- with right and left hands, doing layups, and passing to an open player.

- Defensive skills include defensive stance, rebounding, and help defense.

- Rating systems can vary; make sure all evaluators understand the system.

- Post the final roster after final tryouts are complete. Evaluators discuss and put together the right mix of players.

- AAU teams might have an A and a B team along with several age groups.

- Final cuts should have players' numbers, not names, until all players are confirmed.

- Posting can be done on a Web site or a sheet of paper.

- Coaches should be available for any questions regarding tryouts.

and attentive will catch your eye immediately. These players are eager to learn and will pay attention. If players are attentive, they are easy to coach.

Players who are naturally tall, fast, and strong have somewhat of an advantage. As a coach, you can teach fundamentals to these players. However, players with skills aren't always athletes. Evaluators should evaluate players on a scale from 1 to 5, with 5 being the highest. Offensively, you should look at players who can do both right- and left-hand layups, players who can dribble with both right and left hands, and players

who shoot with the proper hand. Defensively, players should be rated on proper stance, aggressiveness, and rebounding and help defense.

Final Roster

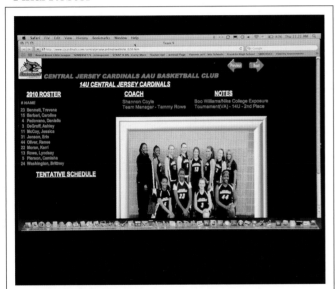

- Your final roster will have the names of all players, coaches, and managers who will represent your team.

- Players like to see their names on a Web site and a team picture.

- The final roster should include players' first and last names, heights, positions, and school names.

- Other important information can be given out to team members but not publicized. Information such as emergency contacts, e-mail addresses, and telephone numbers should be kept private.

Evaluators

- Evaluators should have a basketball background.

- Ask an "outside person" who is not involved in the team but who has a knowledge of the game.

- Do not have parents evaluating. This will cause conflicts.

- Evaluators should not be court coaches. They should sit off to the side.

- Two evaluators with a court coach are sufficient.

185

PICKING ACCORDING TO POSITION
"B" for "best," but also "B" for "balance"

When picking your team, pick a balance of guards and forwards. You don't want a team of all guards or all forwards. Pick six guards and six forwards/centers. A starter and a backup player will be set in all positions. If you do this, you will have a first and a second string, with two remaining players who can be subbed in.

At tryouts you will immediately pick out the taller players. Separate players according to height and divide into one-on-one groups. You will not be able to focus on who the strongest guards and strongest forwards are. After you have an idea of the players you like, create an A team and a B team. Do not tell players you are doing this; they eventually can figure it out on their own. After the separation is made, look for players you're going to keep. The other team will have weaker players on it. Look to see who the best one or two players are on the B team. At this time you can change

Skill Level

- Look for players that can dribble, shoot, and play defense.

- Look for players that are aggressive and go after rebounds.

- Look for team leaders who will encourage other players.

- Look for players that have a sense of how to play the game.

Different Sizes of Players

- Players come in many heights and weights. Players who catch your eye immediately will be the taller players. These players will make up your forward and center positions.

- Smaller players will make up your guard positions.

- Players who are in between the forward and guard positions will be of value because they can play all positions.

- Look for players who are coachable and will play well together.

these two players to the A team in exchange for players who might be on the bubble. Give all players the opportunity to show their skills and the opportunity to play on the A court. Do not divide kids during the first session of tryouts. Kids will get turned off if they aren't picked for the A team and won't come back to the next tryout.

School Team Players

- After a required physical is taken, players may try out for their school team.

- Middle school teams allow sixth-, seventh-, and eighth-graders to try out. Some schools, however, allow only seventh- and eighth-graders to play together, while sixth-graders play on a B-level team.

- Boys' and girls' school teams differ in that the boys' teams tend to get more players to try out than the girls' and will require several days of tryouts. Keep this in mind when picking a team.

AAU Players

- AAU players are picked according to age and grade level.

- AAU rules require players to be of a certain age by a given date.

- AAU teams typically keep between ten and twelve players and play against teams of their age group.

- For example, U10s are fifth grade, U11s are sixth grade, U12s are seventh grade, and U13s are eighth grade.

TRYOUTS: 10–12-YEAR-OLDS

Run a variety of drills to evaluate players' potential

At tryouts you want to run a variety of drills that will showcase your potential players' strengths and weaknesses on the court. Keep it simple and keep it moving when holding tryouts for players ten to twelve years of age.

At the start of tryouts, players should register and receive a number to pin on their back. An index card with a number will do. Gather players in the middle of the floor and explain to them what will take place in tryouts. Your court coaches or

you should warm players up by having them jog around the court. Bring them back in for a quick stretch and then start drill work.

Start tryouts by lining up players on the baseline, five lines of five players in each line. Do not make lines too long. These lines are dribble lines. Have players do different types of dribbles up and down court. Look for players who can dribble with both left and right hands. You should spend about

Four Ways to Keep the Team's Attention

- Keep lectures short.
- Keep drills short and fun.
- Use whistle often.
- Always use lines to do drills to keep organized.

Dribble Lines

- Dribble lines are a great way to see which players can dribble during a tryout.

- Because players are in lines, and only five players are going at a time, you will be able to see the players who keep their heads up and who dribble in a controlled manner.

- Look for players who can use both their right and left hands and can do a crossover dribble.

- Add a jump stop at the end of the dribble lines so you can see who knows how to use their pivot foot.

ten to fifteen minutes on this. The next set of drills should be layups: Full-court layups at full speed. Place half of the players down one end of the court and half down the other end. Players dribble full length and perform a layup, get the rebound, and give to the player waiting in line to go down the opposite end. Players get a lot of turns, and the evaluator will see a lot of players at once.

Court coaches should explain each drill and have a player demonstrate the drill so the other players understand. Defensive slides up the court are good for seeing which players are in shape. At this age group, players don't pass to each other very well, so doing one-on-one, two-on-two, and three-on-three drills allows you to see players better. This forces players to pass to each other.

Layup Lines

- Players should know how to do a layup at this age level.

- The majority of players will be right-handed, so doing a layup on the right side will be easy for them.

- The left-handed layup is an issue at this level. Make sure players dribble with their left hand and lift their left leg to shoot a layup. Players will have a difficult time shooting with their left hand, and that's okay. Allow them to shoot with their right hand until they are comfortable shooting with their left hand.

Game Play

- Playing one-on-one, two-on-two, three-on-three, and a scrimmage game shows a lot about a player.

- Game play separates players who are skilled but who can't function in a game.

- Look for players who move around knowing where to go. Players who are aggressive, who are always around the ball, and who set up other teammates are players who understand the game.

- Tryouts should start with one-on-one and then build up to a full scrimmage.

TRYOUTS: 13–14-YEAR-OLDS
Players should arrive in good physical shape to try out

Players at this age have been through tryouts before. Whether they were on the team the previous year or have been in the program, they clearly know what to expect. Players should arrive in good physical shape and have a medical clearance, especially for a school team.

If you are coaching a school team, separate your tryouts by grade level so that not all grades are on the same day. Bring top players together for two more days of tryouts and then make final cuts. Do not plan to take a certain number at each grade level. Pick the best mix. However, keep in the back of your mind the fact that you will lose players to graduation.

Do not waste tryout time on dribble lines or passing. Instead, incorporate these skills in full-court fast-break drills. A good warm-up drill is a two-on-zero fast break. This works on passing, conditioning, and layups. Then go into three-man weave. You will be surprised how many kids have a

Conditioning Drills

- Any type of conditioning drill that is related to basketball can be used in tryouts.

- Do not have players running for an extended period of time. Instead have them do quick sprints while dribbling or passing quickly down court.

- You will be able to see which players are in shape and which players are better athletes. Look for players who present speed and jumping ability.

Transition Drills

- Transition drills incorporate many skills during tryouts.

- Players who are able to transition from one drill to the next and understand the skills required to perform those drills are valuable players to have on your team.

- Keep in mind that you want players who are ready and able to do more advanced drills. Players try out because they want to learn and be competitive, not because they want to play for recreation.

difficult time with the three-man weave.

Transition now into drills with defense. A two-on-one fast break and a three-on-two allow players to showcase both offensive and defensive skills. If time allows, put in the eleven-man fast break, which is a favorite drill among players. You will be able to see aggressive rebounding and players rotating properly on defense. Toward the end of tryouts, allow at least twenty minutes of scrimmaging. At the end bring players into a huddle and remind them that hard work, hustle, and a good attitude will impress the coach even if

their shooting is off. Also, remind them to not be intimidated by players who made the team last year.

Game Play

- Divide your stronger and weaker players after you have a good idea who belongs where after skill work.

- Have two scrimmages going on so you can see both weaker and stronger players at the same time.

- Your better players on the B court should sub back and forth with the A court. Give players on the "bubble" a chance at both groups. By doing this you can decide who you want to fill the remaining spots on your roster.

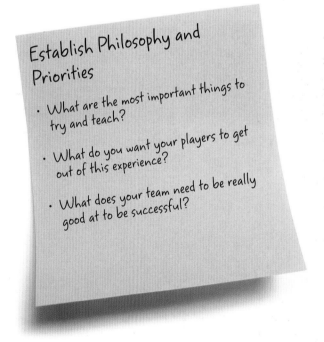

Establish Philosophy and Priorities

- What are the most important things to try and teach?

- What do you want your players to get out of this experience?

- What does your team need to be really good at to be successful?

GYM USE, TIME & STRATEGY
The structure of your practice will determine the success of your team

You have to plan for success and plan your practices just as a teacher creates a lesson plan. Your practice should be like a classroom and you like the teacher. Plan practice in three parts: Preseason drills, in-season drills, and postseason drills. Certain drills, such as ball handling and shooting drills, should be practiced every day. Depending on your schedule,

the amount of practice time you have and what your specific team needs will determine which drills need to be done. A rough rule of thumb is to spend about half the time on individual fundamentals and half the time on team skills. If you're coaching beginner basketball players, then spend more time on skill work.

Gym Time

- Gym time will vary depending on the team you are coaching.

- If you coach a school team, you will typically get two hours of practice and a full-court gym every day. School teams don't practice on weekends.

- Travel teams share gym times if availability of gym space is limited.

- On average, youth teams get one to two days a week to practice.

- Find out from your athletic director if more gym space is available.

Time/Sample Practice

- When scheduling a practice, divide practice into two parts: Skill work and team concepts.

- Skill work can include warm-ups and transition drills. Allow time for taking water breaks in between and stretching in the beginning.

- Drills should last between ten and fifteen minutes and quickly transition into the next drill.

- Team concepts will last longer because of more explanation of plays and mistakes made doing them.

When teaching new drills—or new players, for that matter—teach by progression. Have one drill lead into the next or take it week by week. Don't introduce the eleven-man fast break during the first week of practice. Instead start with a two-on-one fast break and then move to a three-on-two and then an eleven-man fast break. Same goes for teaching new defenses and offenses.

Gym use and time will be factors in setting up your practice plan. Average time for youth players is one hour and a half of practice two times a week. School teams have the advantage of practicing everyday for two hours after school. Don't come into the gym each day without a plan and think you can wing it. Keep a loose-leaf notebook of each of your practices. Take notes during practice so you can refer back, and don't forget to put the date of practice on the notes. Budget your time for each drill. Allow enough time to introduce a new drill and move quickly through old drills.

Scrimmage versus Other Teams

- Bringing other teams in to scrimmage your team is a good idea. Have a controlled scrimmage with no refs so both teams can work on their plays.

- A controlled scrimmage will have its own set of rules. For example, offense might get the ball five possessions in a row, and then offense switches to defense.

- The ball is typically "checked" at the top of the key.

- Both coaches will ref and coach at the same time.

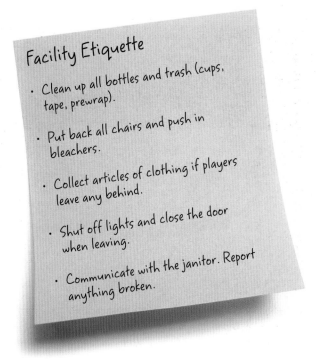

Facility Etiquette
- Clean up all bottles and trash (cups, tape, prewrap).

- Put back all chairs and push in bleachers.

- Collect articles of clothing if players leave any behind.

- Shut off lights and close the door when leaving.

- Communicate with the janitor. Report anything broken.

193

ESSENTIAL PRACTICE PLANNING

A crisp hour-and-a-half training session beats a dragged-out two-hour practice

Select drills that help teach individual and team fundamental skills as well as teach what you try to accomplish or try to correct. You should have a "core" set of selected drills that you use all the time. But allow time to throw in other drills specific to a certain skill. Changing up drills prevents boredom and keeps players' interest. Don't spend half of practice

time on one drill. If players aren't getting the drill or the drill isn't serving its purpose, move to the next drill. Use the drill again the next day with necessary adjustments. Spending too much time on a drill will bore the players, especially if all players aren't involved.

Before practice, stretching exercises should be done.

Warming Up/Stretching

- Warm-up drills and stretching get players' blood flowing and get players ready to participate in harder drills in practice.

- Younger players do not need much stretching because their bodies are already flexible, and they are probably running

around chasing each other anyway before practice. Don't waste too much time on stretching.

- Warm-up drills can be drills that you actually use during game warm-ups. Some teams have a routine of the same drills to get warmed up.

Shooting Drills

- Shooting drills can be done in many ways. You can have players break up into baskets with partners and work on shooting. You can do full-court shooting transition drills that involve the whole team. And finally you can do position breakdown

and do shooting drills tailored to specific positions.

- Whatever shooting drills you do, make sure they serve a purpose and are done in a game-like fashion.

Require players to stretch before the actual practice starts so time isn't wasted. While players are waiting on the sidelines to use the court, stretching should be performed. However, many times players arrive two minutes before practice begins so allow ten minutes of stretching at the beginning of practice. You can discuss your plans for the day or explain which things need to be worked on. Use this time to praise good things that have happened and to give players any important reminders.

· · · · · · · · · · GREEN ● LIGHT · · · · · · · · · ·

End practices on an upbeat note with a drill that builds team spirit. Whether it's a game of knockout, a foul shot to end practice, or a half-court shot by the coach, all these little things help build team spirit. Don't forget to huddle up at the end of practice by bringing hands in together and shouting out a motivational word or phrase.

Defensive Drills

- Many players do not like defensive drills because drills tend to be hard and require players to use leg muscles and stay low.

- Stamina, muscle coordination, good wind, and agility are prerequisites for a good defensive player.

- By doing defensive drills, you are also working on conditioning. Good physical and mental condition allows you to know that players are prepared and that you can count on them to defend.

Plays

- After different plays are introduced, be specific in running plays to go against man and zone. Add a play that can work against both.

- Have one out-of-bounds play, one press break, and one zone defense. Keep it simple. Using too many plays will confuse your players. Often players don't even run the plays.

- Review plays by walking through them first and then add defense.

195

PRACTICE: 6–9-YEAR-OLDS
Have every player do dribbling and ball-handling drills

Practices for this age group require the majority of time on skill work. If you have practice two times a week, I suggest using one of the practices on skill work only. Because of limited practice time and the short attention span of these younger players, keep things simple.

Don't try to accomplish too much. Have a plan and stick to it. At every practice spend ten to fifteen minutes on each skill. For example, fifteen minutes of ball handling and dribbling,

fifteen minutes of passing, fifteen minutes of layups, and fifteen minutes of shooting. The thirty minutes you can spend on game play. "Game play" means one-on-one or two-on-two. Wait until two weeks into practice before you start scrimmaging.

Don't forget to teach footwork to these young players, footwork such as pivoting, triple-threat position, correct footwork for layups, and sliding defense. This area of footwork is

Practice Plan

- For youth players you want to focus on long-term development, not on how many games you win.

- If you try to progress players too quickly, it will hurt them in the long run. You want them to have a solid foundation first.

- Practice should focus on the basic skills, layouts, dribbling, passing, rebounding, and defense.

- At each practice work on two skills throughout the practice. Then pick another two skills the next practice.

Coach Teaching

- Teaching athletic movement skills is critical at this age. Teach these young players how to run, jump, skip, pivot, stop, move, and balance.

- The skills that need to be mastered the most at this level are layups and dribbling. Layups should be practiced with both right

- and left hands while jumping off the proper foot.

- Take time to explain proper footwork so players learn the rules. Teach them how to pivot and jump shoot.

- Teach the triple threat so players understand squaring to the basket.

critical at this age. The correct footwork will help young players advance their skills.

Make drills competitive and fun. Players at this age get excited when they are timed or have to make a certain number of shots. Make the drills have a winner and loser but as a team—never single out an individual. Loser would have to do push-ups or sit-ups or a sprint. To get players to concentrate on foul shooting, if they miss a shot they have to sprint up and back down the court. This simulates game situations and forces players to shoot when they are tired. Finally, make sure all players do dribbling and ball-handing drills. This will help their overall coordination and improve their hands. You can't tell at this age what position these players will grow into.

One-on-one

- One-on-one games are a great way to teach younger players to play.

- Limit their dribbles and pay close attention to them walking and double dribbling. Correct them every time they do it. Give the defense the ball if the offense doesn't follow the

rules. Players will learn the rules because they want to be on offense.

- Play both winners and losers out. This means if a player scores, he stays on offense. Or players switch possession after every made basket.

Fun Games

- Fun games at this level are a great way to end practice. Use the last ten minutes to play fun games.

- Fun games could be knock-out, dribble tag, candyland, and red light-green light.

- Players will walk away from practice with a smile.

- Allow players by vote to pick which fun games they would like to play. You can always mix up the games or make up a new one. Even if the fun games have nothing to do with basketball, kids love games.

197

PRACTICE: 10–12-YEAR-OLDS
At this level of play, team is the name of the game

With a year or two of basketball experience under their belt, players in this age group will be able to understand more of a team game. These players will begin to understand that they are part of a team and become unselfish in their thinking. It's your job to make these players feel a part of a team and to install plays and encourage teamwork.

Practices should still be one hour and thirty minutes: Forty-five minutes of skills work and forty-five minutes of team concepts. Break down players by position when doing skill work so you can tailor drills specific to their position. For example, if you have an assistant coach, you can send players down to one end of the floor so he can work on specific post moves while guards work on specific guard moves down at the other end.

Because practice is limited, try to find out who can dribble and handle the ball. These players will end up being your

Practice Plan

- Many players have had a year of development. This doesn't mean that skill work stops and focus turns to running plays.

- Skill work continues to be taught, and players should start to get comfortable with playing offense and team defense.

- Teach basic cuts to get open and basic screens to free teammates.

- Try to avoid zone defenses. Instead, teach basic man defense. Implement basic footwork and basic principles of man defense.

Skill Work

- With players this age, you should explain more advanced skills.

- Teach backdoor cut, L cut, curl cut, and so forth.

- Continue to focus on shooting form and introduce game-like shots. For

example, teach coming off a screen to shoot.

- Have players pass the ball under pressure. Teach off-the-dribble pass and hook pass into post.

- Teach defense principles but emphasize off-the-ball concepts and rebounding.

point guard and wings. Your taller players at this age will be your forwards and center. Start to install some type of offense set. Keep it simple. A three-out, two-in set will create spacing. A three-out, two-in set is a point guard, left and right wing, and two post players. Teach them the number system. The number system of positions is as follows: "1" is the point, "2" is the right wing, "3" is the left wing, "4" is the right post, and "5" is the left post. Remind players that they are put into this position to create spacing but encourage them to cut and move. At this age level, teach one basic play for man and zone and teach a simple out-of-bounds play. Players will not execute plays at this age anyway. Just let them play.

Spacing

- Do not use any structured or patterned offenses. First get your players comfortable on the court. They will start to figure things out on their own. Your main concern should be to have them move and not stand still.

- After players feel comfortable on the court, teach proper spacing. As they progress, introduce a basic motion offense.

- Play a lot of two-on-two and three-on-three so players get used to getting open and using team concepts.

Foul Shots

- During practice, practice foul shots under game-like conditions.

- Incorporate running after every foul shot missed. Shoot foul shots after doing partner shooting.

- Shoot foul shots as a team at the end of practice. If you have twelve players, set a goal of making six shots. For every shot missed toward the goal, a sprint is done by the team. This stimulates game pressure situations and forces players to concentrate.

PRACTICE: 13–14-YEAR-OLDS

Players of this age can handle advanced drills

This age group will be able to handle advanced drills, team plays, and conditioning. Early in the season do conditioning drills. Remember that you are preparing this age group for high school play, and we all know that high school players go through preseason training. If you're going to make players run, make them do it with a ball. Instead of having them sprint up and down the court, have them speed dribble with a ball. Rather than having them run a suicide,

have them do it with a basketball. By adding a basketball, players can work on two skills at once: Conditioning and dribbling. Not all conditioning drills should be done with a basketball, however. Mixing up conditioning drills keeps kids from hating to run.

Skill work continues throughout the season, but there will be times in practice when you need to prepare your team for a big game or a certain opponent. Work on any special

Practice Plan

• Practices will continue to work on skill work; however, more defensive pressure will be added to drills. Transition drills such as two-on-one, three-on-two, and eleven-man fast break should be done.

• Spend more time on team concepts. Running plays, playing team defense, and rebounding as a team become important.

• Teach players how to get over screens, how to read all options of a play, and how to get teammates involved.

Breakdown

• Break players down into positions. Have all guards together to do specific drills and have forwards together to do post moves.

• Guards will work on fakes and off-the-dribble moves such as behind the back and between the legs.

• Post players will work on rebounding and different moves to the basket. Have an assistant coach pass the ball into post. Teach post defense as well.

situations necessary to play the upcoming opponent, for example, executing a last-second shot play or stalling at the end of a game. You can also refine your own plays. Make adjustments if the other team presses or reconsider how you will defend an opposing team's star player.

By scouting opposing teams, you can tell players about things the opposing teams tend to do, and then make appropriate changes. As the season comes to an end and tournament play approaches, less focus will be spent on skill work and more on team skills for the upcoming game.

Don't overpractice at this time; players can get burned out by the end of the season. Instead have players walk through practices and shoot rebounds. Players will be able to work on their shooting and focus on team concepts. Tournament time is fun for the kids.

Conditioning

- The way basketball is played today, it's one of the most strenuous games, and therefore players must be in top condition.

- Poor conditioning shows up in a player in many ways. When a player begins to tire, her ability to shoot accurately becomes notice- able, her timing is off, and the player she is guarding gets around her.

- Practice conditioning drills both with and without a basketball so players can be in top condition through- out the game.

Special Situations

- Take time to work on special situations. Special situations require specific plays and strategy.

- Work on end-of-quarter strategy, late-game strat- egy, and situations when your team is behind.

- Install last-second shot plays, sideline plays, and plays for "running the clock."

- Be sure players know when to foul and when to call timeouts.

- Have basic rules that every- one is clear on before the game starts and during a timeout.

FOLLOW-UP & REVIEW

"Win" is a three-letter word, but so is "fun"

Unfortunately, we all get caught up in wins and losses. Coaches are remembered for achieving milestones such as career wins and championships. Of course, good coaching will translate into more wins. Teaching fundamentals, developing your program, having passion and dedication, and working hard allow this to happen. But all coaches aren't blessed with talent every year. Great coaching is not always accurately reflected by the win/loss record. Some coaches turn inexperienced kids with poor fundamentals and no confidence into a winning team by season's end. Although they lost more games than they won, they began beating teams that defeated them earlier in the season. These players walked away with a sense of pride and felt good about themselves. Measure the success of your team by how well players learned, developed, improved, and matured to become better players. Make sure these players had fun.

Strength of the Team

- Make a list of the weaknesses and strengths of your team. Break it down into two categories of practice and games.

- Review your notes and write a summary of the season.

- Collect newspaper articles, game film, or any other keepsakes.

- Don't forget to collect all uniforms and turn in any end-of-the-year reports.

- Thank all parents, players, administrators, managers, and assistant coaches.

Weaknesses of the Team

- There will be improvement needed in your team each year.

- Some years, the weakness of your team will be different than other years.

- Break the season into three parts: Beginning, middle, and end.

- Assess what weaknesses of the team continue throughout the season.

- Many teams improve as the season progresses, but a constant weakness that continues throughout the season must be addressed.

As you reflect on your season, make notes of the positives and negatives and things that need to be changed for the next year. Even if you had a winning record and walked away with a championship, improvements can be made. Players graduate, players move, and some players decide not to come back. Nothing is guaranteed for the next year. Keep in touch with your players after the season. Suggest that they play AAU spring ball or participate in a summer camp. Provide them with an off-season training program or have open gym time once in awhile for the players to shoot.

Feedback/Gathering

- Always end the season on a positive note, even if you feel the season didn't go as planned. Let players know you care and you appreciate their efforts.

- A pizza party is always the safest bet. Whether it's the last practice or last game, have something afterward to say "Thank you."

- Invite the parents and any other people involved in helping your team.

- Talk about the positives of the season and maybe some personal memories.

Off-season/Open Gym

- Develop an off-season workout plan of skill work and conditioning for your players. Make it a general plan of working on ball handling, shooting, and conditioning.

- Make it simple and clear-cut and tailor the workout so players can do it by themselves.

- Offer open gyms maybe twice a month and provide players with information on upcoming camps and clinics.

- Encourage players to attend different training programs so they can learn from different coaches.

STARTING LINEUP
It's not who starts the game; it's who finishes

The term "starting lineup" simply means the five players starting the game. Typically these players are your five best players or the five players who work well together. At the high school level it's often the same starters with a change here and there. When you coach a youth team, the starting five shouldn't be made into a big deal. With youth teams let all your players take turns starting. This allows players to feel a part of the team and gives everyone an opportunity.

However, it's a good idea to start three of your best players and to rotate the other two. Another way to rotate players is to have them start the second half. This also develops team chemistry.

Some leagues have standard substitution patterns in which they sub every four minutes. This allows for different players to start each quarter. In AAU play often there are four games in one weekend. This gives you some opportunities to start

Preparation

- The coach is responsible for many things on game day.

- The coach needs to bring the basketballs, scorebook, first-aid kit, and clipboard to the game.

- Before the start of the game, a certain routine should be followed. Players

should arrive early to the game and begin to stretch and get their uniform and sneakers on.

- Coaches should know in advance any special rules such as those relating to running clocks and number of timeouts.

Starting Five

- If you are coaching youth basketball in which everyone is supposed to play, then choosing a starting lineup shouldn't be difficult.

- The starting lineup can be switched from game to game and be switched at halftime.

- It's a good rule of thumb to start your two best players and never sub all your weaker players in together. When this happens, it's hard for them to have success. If your league requires sub-bing at a certain time, then make sure you have strong players in each group.

different players. Some leagues announce the starting lineup. The players sit on the bench and the rest of the players line up across from each other. When a starter is announced he runs through the line and slaps his teammates' hands and runs to the middle of the floor. Each starter repeats the process. Players love it, and it gets them excited to play. Fans also clap at this time to cheer their team on.

Starting Five School Team

- Older players value the job of starting more than younger players do. It means more to them, and for some players it really can have an effect on play. Coaches must stress to these players who have a hard time when they don't start that it's important who finishes the game.

- Players enjoy hearing their name called on the loud speaker as the starting lineup is announced. It gets players pumped for the game.

Game Day Reminders

- Yelling at players is unnecessary. Never embarrass a player.

- Be on good terms with the referee and introduce yourself and shake hands before the game.

- Have an end-of-the-game strategy.

- Show good sportsmanship.

- Motivate players and be a positive coach. Be vocal in encouraging players and telling them plays and strategies.

SUBSTITUTION PATTERN

Be consistent, be fair, and let players earn their playing time

Each coach has her own way of substituting players. Some coaches believe in a system of five in and five out. Some coaches have to follow league rules, and some coaches sub based on the flow of the game. Whatever your method is, players must be subbed.

There are several reasons why players need to be subbed. Players who get into foul trouble, especially during the first half, need to come out so they don't pick up extra fouls and are unable to play the rest of the game. After a player picks up his second foul, adjustments need to be made depending on when he picks up his second foul. A good time to sub players in is three to four minutes into the quarter. At this time you will be able to see who on the court needs a sub because they are getting fatigued or not playing well. Subbing one or two players at this time is ideal. And finally, if a player gets hurt and needs a sub immediately, then let a sub take his place.

Subbing

- Subbing is done for several reasons. It's important for a coach to be aware of these reasons, including because a player is in foul trouble, a player is hurt or tired, and a player isn't doing the job.

- Make sure the player going in knows which player he is subbing in for and which opponent he is guarding.

- Players can sub only during a dead ball.

- Subbing in on a foul shot happens after the first foul shot.

Sub Pattern

- Rely on your assistant coaches to help you handle substitution patterns. If you have only six players, then it's easy to handle. Teams that have over ten players should have an assistant coach keeping track of playing time.

- As a coach, you can easily get caught up in the game and forget to sub. Try your best to get all players in. As players get older, they should learn to earn their playing time and not expect everything to be given to them.

Remind players who are on the bench to look at which defense is played and which offense is run. When it's time for a player to go into the game, he must report to the scorer's table. He waits until a ref signals him into the game. At this time the player runs over to the other player and lets him know he is coming in for that player. The player coming out should tell the opponent. The player who comes out should sit next to the coach to go over positives and negatives of his play. Be aware of league rules about substitution patterns. Often in the fourth quarter, leagues don't allow best players to play.

Hurt Player

- When a player is hurt, the ref will make a decision based on the play of the game whether to stop play.

- If a player gets hurt being fouled, then play is auto-matically stopped. The ref will signal the coach or trainer onto the court to help the hurt player.

- If a player gets hurt during a fast break, the ref will let the play continue and then wait for a dead ball.

- If a player gets hurt and the play is casual, the ref will stop the game. This is called an "official timeout." Refs can do this at anytime during the game.

Fouled-out Player

- In all basketball games except professional games, when a player gets five fouls he has to come out of the game.

- Coaches must warn players and must be notified by the scorekeeper when a player is in foul trouble.

- When a player fouls out, the coach has a minute to decide whom to put into the game.

- Players who get called for a technical foul will be issued a personal foul as well.

ACTUAL GAME PLAN

A game-time routine should be followed whether your team is 0–10 or 10–0

Every coach has his way of preparing for game day. Game day is an important time for coaches and players to get comfortable with the situation and to focus on the job to be done. Be organized and make sure everyone around you is as well. Allow enough time to arrive at the gym: At least forty-five minutes prior is ideal. Rushing around at the last minute creates a disorganized, frantic mood. This upsets players and parents. You want players and coaching staff to be relaxed and calm as the game starts.

There are necessary things to do before each game. Review with your assistants (if you have them) the starting lineup, sub patterns, and strategies of the game. Make sure players'

Pregame Talk

- Pregame talk is used to get players to focus and to explain and review the upcoming game to them.

- Set a calm tone. Don't make players nervous. Taking a business-like approach is better than getting your team fired up. Kids already know that it's a big game.

- It's how you prepare and how you work on fundamentals and team skills that really count.

- Players should not worry about playing good or bad, winning or losing. They need to just go out and do their job.

Warm-ups

- Warm-up time will vary depending on where your team is playing. If you're in a league in which games are played all day, expect ten minutes of warm-up time. If your team is playing after school, and you're traveling to another school, expect twenty minutes of warm-up time.

- Warm-ups are just that, a way to get players' bodies warmed up, loose, and ready to play. Players will sweat a little and work on shots they will take during the game.

208

numbers are in both scorebooks. A technical foul could result if players are not in the books. Make sure your team has chairs or a bench to sit out on. Have your clipboard handy at all times. The medical kit and water bottles should be placed at the end of the bench. Remind players to put their names on their water bottles.

If you're at a school where you have access to a locker room, make use of it. Typically the team meeting before the game takes place in a gym corner or in the hallway. Teams that are able to use a locker room before and after the game should do so. The locker room is a place to go over game strategies, dress for the game, and mentally prepare for the game.

Warm-ups usually last about ten minutes, depending on if other teams are playing before and after. With one minute left in warm-ups, bring your team over to get settled to play the game. Members of the starting lineup and the other players will huddle around the coach. At this time you will go over assignments and team strategies.

Bench Cheering

- Players on the bench are expected to cheer for their teammates on the floor.

- Typically six to seven players are sitting on the bench.

- When a player comes out of the game, players should move down and allow the player coming out to sit next to the coach. Players should also stand up for the player coming out or put a hand out to be high-fived.

- Bench players should be cheering throughout the game.

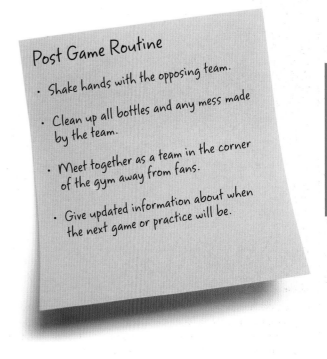

Post Game Routine

- Shake hands with the opposing team.

- Clean up all bottles and any mess made by the team.

- Meet together as a team in the corner of the gym away from fans.

- Give updated information about when the next game or practice will be.

SCOUTING OTHER TEAMS

Courtside coaching can greatly influence the outcome of a game, especially a close game

Preparing for the game at the youth level involves more preparation to better the players you have. As players get older, more scouting and watching game film are necessary.

At the youth level find out which offensive players are the best and which defense the other team tends to play. Certain leagues don't allow teams to press until the last quarter, so

for three quarters you will be dealing with half-court sets.

As the season progresses, you will learn which teams are in your league. Many times you play a team twice, so you can be more prepared the second time around. A good habit to get into is taking notes right after watching a team play. Save the notes, so you can refer back to them. Practice is a good

Scouting

- Scouting requires you to go out and watch the other team play or to watch the team on game film.

- Make sure you take notes during the game. Write down who the team's starters are and who comes in for them. Youth leagues sub every four minutes, so look

- to see what best players they put in after the substitution takes place.

- You can develop a game plan that will favor your strengths and attack their weaknesses.

Other Team Plays

- Youth teams do not run elaborate plays and don't run a lot of plays.

- As a coach, you will be able to see what they typically run. Look for certain names of plays being called or signals given.

- Don't forget about the

- out-of-bounds plays and special plays.

- One important thing to remember is not to change your game plan that you do successfully to something else solely to stop your opponents. Make the opponents change their style to try to stop you.

time to discuss with your players what the other team runs. At this time you can explain to your players which defense the other team runs and which players are good. You can teach your players how to guard their best player and maybe incorporate a special defense. Box-and-one defense works many times against youth teams, particularly if one player is outstanding.

If you have never played the team before and have no prior information, try watching the opponents during warm-ups. Warm-ups will not give you a true assessment, but at least you can get an idea about players who somewhat have a clue. During the first few minutes try to learn early who their best players are and what style of tempo they play. After you know this you can make quick adjustments in a timeout or end of the first quarter. Most importantly, if your team is prepared and ready to play, then a few adjustments can be made throughout the game. Preparation is the key to winning games.

Presenting to Team

- When presenting the scouting report, explain different players' strengths and weaknesses. Give a brief description of the players and what they like to do.

- Break down guards and post play so your team knows the positions that players play.

- Give specific defense assignments so each player knows his role exactly and whom he will be responsible for guarding.

- Make sure players ask questions during practice. Asking during the game will be too late.

Scout Team

- Older teams sometimes have a scout team. A scout team is five players acting like the opponents' team. These five players try to play like the opponents, showing the same characteristics and doing what the opponents would do during the game.

- The scout team runs the opponents' exact plays and incorporates their characteristics.

- Having a scout team is a good way to prepare because it incorporates game-like situations.

HALFTIME ADJUSTMENTS
Set the game tempo to the style that best suits your team

The best time to make adjustments during the game is at halftime. During this time players are focused, and you're not being rushed. You can draw up diagrams on the chalkboard or clipboard and really go over what adjustments need to be made. During halftime you can demonstrate on the court where players should be and actually walk them through.

Both positive and negative comments should be given at this time. Take time to compliment players. If you give criticism, do it in a manner that offers a way to fix the problem. Screaming at kids during halftime will get nothing accomplished. Instead use the time to explain what needs to be done in the second half. If your team is losing, a few words of encouragement can get the kids motivated. If you're getting blown out, set a few goals that you would like to see achieved in the second half. Let's face it: If you're getting beat by over twenty-five points, clearly the other team is better.

Halftime Talk

- Halftime talk is a time to make quick adjustments and let players know the positives and negatives of the first half.

- Have players sit with water bottles and listen to you. Make sure compliments are given and review what is working for your team.

- Set small goals to be accomplished during the second half of play.

- Ask players if they have any comments they would like to share. Don't let your players complain or try to make excuses.

Chalk Talk

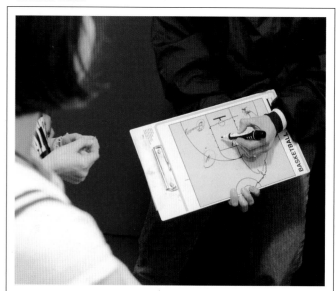

- "Chalk talk" means discussion of diagram plays on the chalkboard.

- Some players are better learners when they see a play diagrammed for them on the board.

- Coaches can show what the opponents are doing on offense and how to stop them.

- Write down the jersey numbers of the opponents and write down their strengths and weaknesses as reminders. This can be done before the game so players can see them again at halftime.

Halftime is also a good time for players to rest, go to the rest room, and fix any uniform equipment. Give players the option to shoot around at halftime. Halftime is only five to ten minutes long. Shooting around won't get so much accomplished but allows players that option to make adjustments on their shots.

Whether it is halftime or a timeout, keep your speech to the point and simple. Kids won't remember a lot—usually just the last thing you say. Use timeouts wisely. Remember that at the end of each quarter is a free timeout. Use timeouts to break the opponents' momentum. Ideally, save your timeouts if a game is close so you can use them toward the end.

Halftime Shooting

- Halftime shooting can be used as a time to make adjustments on players' shots. Players who are frustrated with their shooting during the first half can work on making the necessary correction. Get a teammate to rebound for the player, and the player should shoot the ball in close.

- If your team struggles with shooting, go back to basic warm-up drills to get players to refocus.

- Time is limited during halftime, so use it wisely.

What Coaches Should Do During Halftime:

- Check your book to see who is in foul trouble on both teams.

- Talk to assistant coaches about any adjustments needed.

- Talk to players individually, if need be.

- Take a small break yourself (get a drink, go to the bathroom, etc.).

GAME ATTIRE
Look and act professional both on and off the court

Looking and feeling good are important for both coaches and players. Representing your team and conducting yourself in the proper manner can go a long way. Whether the game is home or away, proper game attire is a must.

As a staff, discuss what should be worn while coaching games. Coaches can all wear team logo shirts with khaki pants or collared shirts. A coach can wear a shirt and tie if he wishes. Coaches like to get dressed up when there's a big

game. Female coaches should avoid wearing short skirts. Although skirts are fine, they tend to be uncomfortable. Instead wear a nice top and a pair of pants. Make sure shirts are tucked in and sneakers or shoes are clean. A nice jogging suit can also be worn.

Players' uniforms must all match. Remind players to wear the same color of tank top underneath if they want to. Some teams like wearing the same sneakers or the same-colored

Coaches

- Coaches should carry themselves in a professional manner. That goes for assistant coaches and parents as well.

- Make sure you coach in a controlled manner. Screaming and yelling at your players will get you nowhere.

- Know when to stand up and sit down. Assistant coaches should be sitting down at all times.

- Wins and losses aren't important at this age; getting your kids better at playing and understanding the game is.

Players

- Before a game starts, referees will ask for captains from each team to meet at half court to go over rules or issues before the game starts.

- Captains can be two players on your team who show leadership qualities. These

- players are usually the older players on the team.

- If you're undecided as to captains, have players take turns being captains.

- Good sportsmanship is required at all times by all players.

sneakers. Sneakers usually match the team's colors. The team members must decide before the season so players aren't left out. Shooting shirt, bags, and jackets are optional but a nice way to look professional. Again, decide as a team if extra gear is possible. Players might have to pay extra money to do this. Leagues and school teams usually provide just uniforms and practice jerseys.

Many times there isn't a place to change into a uniform. Uniforms should be worn under a jogging suit or sweatpants and game sneakers brought to the game in a bag. Benches need to be cleared of players' bags and water bottles. Shooting shirts and warm-up pants are optional. Socks are typically worn to midcalf. Sweat bands again are optional but useful to wipe sweat.

Game Uniform

- All players will wear the same game uniform. Uniforms must have legible numbers on them. All uniforms must be tucked in.

- Players can wear any type of sneakers as long as they are basketball sneakers. Some teams wear the same sneakers. Players like to wear midcalf socks.

- Girls pull their hair back in a ponytail and sometimes wear a prewrap on their head as a headband.

- Some uniforms have players' last name on the backs. All uniforms will have the name of the team on the front.

Taping

- Each player has a different way of preparing himself for the game. Some players need to get taped before the game. Players typically get their ankles or their fingers taped.

- If a trainer is available, then the trainer will do it; if not, this must be done by the player alone or with help from a parent.

- Many players wear laced-up ankle braces because they are easier than tape.

215

DRILLS FOR INDIVIDUAL WORKOUTS

Players should be creative and develop coordination and stamina

Players need to work on their game throughout the season. Working out individually will help players improve in all areas of their game. Individual workouts will vary during different parts of the season. There is off-season training, in-season training, and a conditioning program to go along with skill work.

Individual workouts are those that players do on their own to improve their game. Individual workouts are a combination of drills that are done at game speed. It is important to do these drills at game-like intensity and to move from one drill to the next. Shooting around for three hours will not improve players, however, doing an intense game-speed one-hour workout will. Players need to understand that skills develop gradually over time with consistent practice and effort. Don't expect to see quick results. Players need to be committed to the workouts. Consistency is the key for self-improvement.

Form Shooting

- Hands down this is the best shooting drill to work on acquiring proper technique and on fixing players' form.

- A player starts with his feet shoulder width apart. The player brings the ball up to the shooting pocket. The nonshooting hand is not behind the player's back; instead it is up in the shooting pocket but off the ball (this is realistic).

- Players do not shoot with the opposite hand behind the back. By having the nonshooting hand in proper position, the player understands where the hand should ultimately be.

X-out

- The player starts with the ball at the elbow. The player is timed for thirty seconds, forty-five seconds, or one minute.

- The player dribbles full speed toward the basket for a layup. She gets the rebound and quickly dribbles to the opposite elbow. She turns quickly and dribbles in for a left-handed layup. The player then goes back to the right-handed layup and repeats both sides.

- Players should get seven made layups in thirty seconds.

Basketball is a sport of interval training, so workouts should be structured in the same way. Players should mimic workouts with short bursts of activity. Focus should be on both weaknesses and strengths. Plan workouts and keep a journal of recorded results, so progression is tracked.

Players need to train their minds as well as their bodies. Players need to make smart decisions by anticipating and seeing opportunities. Because individual workouts are done with one player, players should keep their minds active by imagining plays and training as if they were in a game.

Skills are developed over time. Few players are able to master a skill without working on it. Learning steps need to be acquired first before a skill is perfected. Remind players not to get discouraged.

Speed Shooting

- Speed shooting is a great drill for working against clock, in pressure situations or for conditioning. Players are timed for one minute.

- Drill can be done in two ways: Toss and catch or off the dribble. The player shoots the ball, runs in for the rebound, dribbles out to any spot on the floor, tosses the ball to herself, and shoots. The player continues this for one minute. She tries to get ten made shots in one minute.

- Off the dribble is done the same way; however, player shoots off dribble instead of tossing to herself.

Box Hits

- The player starts on the baseline with the ball. He dribbles to the elbow and does a hesitation move, then dribbles across to the opposite elbow and does another hesitation move. He then dribbles in for a layup. He repeats this pattern ten times or for one minute.

- Players can use different moves at each elbow and can also shoot jump shots instead of layups.

- This drill is called "box hits" because players will dribble in a box pattern.

DRILLS FOR ONE PLAYER
An extra player can lend two helping hands

These drills are for a single player with a rebounder. Having a rebounder to work with lets a player take many more shots. Whether it's a coach, personal trainer, family member, or a friend, having a person rebound is a bonus. Rebounders are important because they are able to get the rebound quickly out for another shot right away. The rebounder can tell you any corrections that might be helpful to the player as he does the drill. Rebounders can provide players

with encouragement and push them when they are tired. Rebounders can time certain drills and count shots made. They can also record different drills.

Several drills can be done throughout the season with or without a rebounder. As a coach, always offer to rebound for a player, especially if the player comes early or stays late to practice. This time allows for any correction to be made to a player's game and for an opportunity to get to know

KNACK COACHING YOUTH BASKETBALL

Fast Feet

- Players start at the foul line and move their feet in a fast, stuttering manner.

- Rebounders throw the ball to the right of shooter. Shooter reacts to ball, picks up ball, and shoots. After player shoots, he goes back to the original spot and continues doing fast feet.

- Rebounder then throws the ball to the left of the shooter. Shooter picks up the ball and shoots again. This continues.

- Player can switch spots by going to the wing positions, and rebounder can throw the ball wherever he wants for a quick reaction.

Curl Cuts

- Curl cuts force players to come into their shots.

- Passer starts at the top of the key with a ball. Shooter starts on the box and curls out to the elbow area. Passer passes the ball to the shooter. Shooter shoots and gets the rebound and passes back to the passer.

- Shooter does seven curl cuts on the right side. Then he moves to the left side and does five curl cuts.

- Then he moves back to the right side and does three curl cuts and then finishes with one curl cut on the left side.

your players. Managers and assistant coaches are good to rebound and pass, especially for the younger players. Drills get done more quickly and more accurately if coaches pass and rebound.

Players must feel comfortable with the person who rebounds for them. A good rapport will allow for players to progress and trust in the rebounder. If a player is doing a drill with another player, the two simply take turns doing the drill and rebounding.

Right/Left

- This is a basic shooting drill that works on taking a big step to the left and right sides to pull up for a jump shot.

- Player starts with the ball at the top of the key and takes a big step to the right and shoots a jump shot. She then goes back to the middle, receives the ball from the rebounder, and quickly goes to the left. Player should take ten to fifteen shots.

- After the player is done at the top of the key, she should move to the wing area and do the same drill.

Slide Chase

- Passer starts with the ball in the wing area. Shooter starts in a defensive stance and slides out to the passer and touches the ball.

- Passer throws the ball over the shooter's head. Shooter chases down the ball and shoots a layup.

- Shooter then passes the ball back out to the passer and repeats the process. Passer moves to a different location on the court.

- This drill is good for conditioning, reaction, and defensive slides.

DRILLS FOR TWO PLAYERS

Pairing provides a workout on both offense and defense

Players who wish to train with another player should do so with a player of equal ability or age level. Players should choose a partner who is competitive, hard working, and committed. Several drills can involve two players at the same time, and several drills can be done in which one player goes through a series of drills while the other rebounds, and then they switch. Having two players allows for one player to play defense so both offensive and defensive skills can be learned.

During the season break players into baskets to work on skills with another player. Gyms typically have six baskets, and teams are usually made up of twelve players. Putting two players at each basket and having all players going through the same set of drills accomplishes a lot in practice. Match players up according to position, especially with the younger players. You don't want players overmatched because of size and physical ability. In practice all players should start at the

Pass Replace

- One player starts with the ball under the basket. The other is at the foul line. The player with the ball throws it out to the foul line player, who shoots the ball. The player who passed the ball runs by the shooter with her hands up and jumps to put light pressure on the shooter.

- Time players for one minute. Ten shots should be made together.

- Change spots on the floor. Go to both wing areas.

Pass Relocate

- This drill is similar to pass and replace; however, players will relocate to a different spot instead of staying stationary in the same spot.

- After a player passes the ball to the shooter, she relocates to a different spot on the court. The shooter must get the rebound and

find the other player. After the ball is passed again, the shooter relocates. Drill continues for one minute.

- Players can add a dribble going right or left.

same time when doing a timed drill. The coach will blow the whistle to indicate start time.

The player who is waiting will count and encourage the other player participating in the drill. For example, if players are being timed for one minute, the partner will count how many shots were made. Several shooting drills can be done in which both players participate and count shots made together. Players love to be competitive, so having them count allows them to react quickly and compete against other team members. This also gets players to encourage

each other. Kids also love to play one-on-on[...] other. Playing small games up to five points a[...] to work on both offensive and defensive skills [...] different moves from one another.

Two-ball Shooting

- Player starts with the ball at the foul line; the passer also has a ball and is off to the side of the shooter.

- Shooter shoots and gets another ball immediately from the passer. Rebounder quickly gets the ball to the passer.

- Shooter takes twenty shots. After twenty shots, switch shooters.

Shooter Rebounder Passer

- Shooter starts in a corner with the ball. Passer has another ball on top of the key. Rebounder is under the basket.

- Shooter is timed for one minute. After shooter shoots she runs up to wing area and receives a pass from the passer. Shooter

shoots again and then goes back to the corner.

- After a minute is up the shooter becomes the rebounder, rebounder becomes the passer, and passer becomes the shooter.

- Each player gets one minute to shoot. Switch court sides.

CONDITIONING DRILLS WITH BALL
These exercises should be fun, creative, and useful

I'm a believer in conditioning by practicing drills, not just running. A combination of both, however, is necessary. Players will condition their bodies by going through drills and doing sprints, defensive slides, and game play. At the youth level kids don't tire easily. They enjoy running around. Channel their energy into a drill that requires running but also teaches the proper skill.

At the start of the season, more focus should be placed on conditioning the players for the upcoming season. Conditioning will happen by having players participate in many transition drills that require them to run up and down the court. Drills that are timed for the team to accomplish a certain goal force players to move more quickly. If players understand that they are running for a purpose and not just running because they messed up a drill or have to do suicides at the end of practice, they will push themselves harder. Do not waste too

Slide Shots

- Player starts in the corner and slides to wing area. Player receives ball, shoots, then runs back to start in the same spot and then slides again.

- Player can slide anywhere on court into a shot. Make sure players stay low and slide and don't gallop.

Younger players have a tendency to gallop and crisscross their feet.

- This is a great drill for conditioning and staying low to receive a pass to shoot.

Dribble Shots

- Player starts with the ball on the baseline, her back to the foul line.

- Player dribbles the ball while moving backward. After the player reaches the foul line, she takes one big dribble forward into the basket for a layup.

- This drill works on foot speed, dribbling, and conditioning.

- Player can also move farther back by crossing the three-point line, then dribbling forward into a jump shot.

much time doing the same boring conditioning drills. Mix up the drills and make conditioning fun and creative for the players. Have players determine if they run or not in certain drills. If they don't accomplish a certain goal set for them, for example, the players have to make a certain number of shots in the time allowed, and then they have to run.

Players who condition themselves on their own besides during their regular practice time can do so by running 2 to 3 miles along with various sprint workouts. Jumping rope and doing push-ups and sit-ups can also be done throughout the season, not just in the preseason to keep in top form.

Players can do individual workouts by sprinting in to get rebounds, sliding into shots, and sprinting to the sidelines back into a shot. This will get players in shape and give them practice under game-like conditions.

Sprint Shots

- Player starts at the sideline and sprints to the elbow. He receives a pass and shoots. Player then sprints to the opposite sideline, touches it, and sprints to the opposite elbow to shoot. Player continues to sprint and touch sidelines.

- Sprinting drills can be done anywhere on the court. The player can sprint to half court and then into a shot. Or the player can sprint to full court, receive the ball, make a move, and then shoot.

- Coaches can be creative with sprinting into shots.

Full-court Roll

- In a full-court roll a player starts on the baseline and faces outward with the ball on the ground between her legs. Player rolls the ball down court, keeping it in between her legs.

- After the player reaches half court, she picks up the ball and dribbles in for a layup.

- She then gets the rebound and rolls the ball down to the other end.

- This drill should be done with thirteen- to fourteen-year-olds.

USE OF OTHER EQUIPMENT
Training devices can aid in the development of team and players

Several training devices can be used in the development of players, starting, of course, with the basketball itself. Several variations of a ball can be used to improve dribbling.

There is a big ball, which is a large version of the traditional ball but is the same weight. There is a weighted basketball, which is the same size but is heavier. These balls are able to be dribbled and shot. And the last training device is a simple tennis ball. A tennis ball is hard to control because it is small but great for developing hand-eye coordination.

Shooting devices vary depending on the problem that needs to be worked on. There are devices that help if a shooter turns his left hand, doesn't follow through, or drops his hand. Devices can be purchased online. A shooting gun machine can be used by players if available in a gym or training facility. This machine passes out basketballs at different speeds and is useful in getting many shots in over a period of time.

Ball in Chair

- A chair is useful in any practice at any level. There will more than likely be a chair in a gym for use during practice.

- A chair serves as a defender or screener and will hold a ball.

- Many drills can be done using a chair. One good drill is to place a ball in the chair and have players run up to take it out and shoot. Players can do a curl cut and L cut. This forces players to shoot with an object in front of them and to stay low to pick up the ball.

Goal Shooting

- Having a device for a player to shoot over blocks a player's vision and forces him to shoot under game-like conditions.

- A soccer goal turned upward can be used, as well as any other piece of equipment that is tall enough to block a player's vision.

- Having something in front of the player forces her to not jump forward. Younger players have a tendency to do this because they can't reach the basket.

Rebounding pads, jump soles, and the jump shooter are devices that help improve all parts of a player's game. Rebounding pads are used by coaches to make contact with players as they go up for their shots or to contact them when they drive through the lane. Jump soles are sneakers worn to build up players' calf muscles to enable players to jump higher. These sneakers are worn during individual training sessions, not during games. The jump shooter training device forces players to jump at their peak by making them shoot over a device that blocks the shooters' vision. These devices can be purchased by a coach, a school program, or a player. These training devices can be used throughout the season.

Pads

- Rebounding pads are used on players going up for rebounds and driving through the lane area.

- Coaches or managers hold pads by a strap on the back.

- Coaches will make contact with players by hitting them with the pads in the shoulder and chest areas.

- This forces players to go up strong and make contact. It also forces players to try to get a one-on-one shot.

Gloves

- Winter gloves are used to make drills harder for players. The gloves are slippery, and movement is limited.

- Wearing mittens makes it harder for players to handle the ball because the fingers don't move as much. Regular gloves allow for movement, but the gloves are still slippery.

- Dribbling drills should be done both with and without gloves.

- Gloves should be worn by more advanced players.

OFF-SEASON DRILLS

Players need to improve in their game during the off-season

During the off-season, the more advanced player should practice at least five times a week on their own, along with participating in AAU summer leagues and camps. Younger to middle-aged players should participate in at least two weeks of camp and work on their skills three times a week. Younger kids will get better playing many games of one-on-one and two-on-two in the neighborhood.

Younger players will also benefit from attending two to

three weeks of camp. Typically there isn't a summer league for these players, and travel leagues stop in March. Many of the young players are still participating in other sports, so this takes up much of their time. Middle-aged players have the opportunity to play Amateur Athletic Union, which is one of the largest, nonprofit, volunteer sports organizations in the United States.

AAU typically starts at age nine. Middle-aged players really

Dribble Touches

- Dribble touches, or suicides, are good for interval training.

- Player starts on the baseline with the ball. She dribbles full speed to the foul line, touches the line with her hand, and dribbles back to the baseline. Then she dribbles to half court,

  touches the line, dribbles back, dribbles to the opposite foul line, dribbles to the baseline, and returns to the start position.

- This drill can also be done without a basketball.

Ankle Dribbles

- Ankle dribbles help to improve players' dribbling.

- Player starts on the baseline facing inward. Ball is on the side of the player's body right next to her ankle. Player slides while dribbling the ball near to the ankle and at ankle level.

- Player dribbles across the baseline, up the sideline, across half court, and down the sideline to the start position.

- This drill is for more advanced players.

begin training around the seventh grade and continue throughout high school.

An off-season workout program for advanced players should include the following elements: Skill work, conditioning, and game play. Players should do one hour a day of game-like skill work. This includes shooting, dribbling, rebounding, and playing defense. Players should make up a routine schedule including shooting foul shots in between sets. Three days a week should include conditioning in addition to the skill workouts. Conditioning should consist of running 2 to 3 miles, jumping rope, and doing some type of sprint workout. Players can do weights if they are entering high school. Middle-aged players are always safe with doing push-ups and sit-ups to increase strength. Game play should be incorporated into the workout by playing one-on-one and two-on-two. Pickup games are valuable because they teach kids to develop skills on their own.

Speed Shooting

- Speed shooting can be done in many ways in one-minute or two-minute spans of time.

- Player shoots the ball and sprints in for the rebound. She dribbles out and shoots again. The player can add a dribble move or toss the ball in for a shot. The player can go anywhere on the court and can also move out to the three-point line and mix up the shots.

- This drill can be done numerous times during a workout.

Jumping Rope

- Jumping rope is great for conditioning and working on foot speed.

- Players can jump rope before a workout. They can jump for two minutes, rest for a minute, and then continue.

- Players can jump off of two feet or one foot or alternate.

- Jumping rope is fun for all ages. Players really enjoy it and forget they are even conditioning.

- It's great for kids who are heavy footed or don't like to jump.

CAMPS, TRAINING & TOURNAMENTS

Pick a camp, clinic, trainer, and a tournament based on the needs of the player and the team. Look for reputable programs throughout your area.

Local Camps and Clinics

Across your state you will be able to find numerous basketball camps at local high schools, colleges, and basketball facilities. These camps are run by coaches who coach their high school team or by companies that provide a few weeks of basketball throughout the year. Brochures and e-mail will provide you with information about dates and events. Many colleges provide overnight camps as well. Two sites to get information about camps include: www.girlsbasketballcamps .com and www.ussportscamps.com/basketball.

Training

Professional shooting coaches are available throughout the seaso to train players on an individual basis. These trainers can teach at basketball facility or at a local gym. Research your trainer to ma sure you are getting the best for your dollar. Typical trainers cost $ to $100 per hour. Trainers also offer group lessons as well as trainin an entire team. For personal training visit: www.cjcardinals.com.

Tournaments

If you're interested in continuing your season or coaching AAU, se eral weekend tournaments go on throughout the year. The offic Web site that will provide you with a state-by-state selection of tou naments throughout the year is: www.acahoops.com.

Web Sites

Player and coaches should make use of the Internet to get inform tion on basketball. Sites with information on various topics, such retailers, drills, training devices, and camps, can be found on the We

Gear

Basketball Gear
www.basketballgear.com

Eastbay
www.eastbay.com

Nike
www.nike.com

Sports Authority
www.sportsauthority.com

Under Armour
www.underarmour.com

Basketball Drills
www.best-basketball.com
www.breakthroughbasketball.com
www.guidetocoachingbasketball.com

Basketball Scouting Services
www.bluestarbb.com (girls)
www.hoopgroup.com (boys)
www.hoopgurlz.com
www.mcdonaldsallamerican.com

Training Devices
www.jumpusa.com
www.kbacoach.com

Coaches
www.campofchamps.com
www.coachesclipboard.net
www.weplay.com

WOMEN'S NATIONAL BASKETBALL ASSOCIATION (WNBA)

The WNBA is a women's professional basketball league in the United States. It's currently composed of twelve teams. The league was found in 1996 as the women's counterpart to the National Basketball Association (NBA). The regular season is played from May to August, with playoffs in September. For more information on teams and individual players, visit the Web site: www.wnba.com.

Teams in the Eastern Division
Atlanta Dream
Chicago Sky
Connecticut Sun
Indiana Fever
New York Liberty
Washington Mystics

Teams in the Western Division
Los Angeles Sparks
Minnesota Lynx
Phoenix Mercury
San Antonio Silver Stars
Seattle Storm
Tulsa Shock

NATIONAL BASKETBALL ASSOCIATION (NBA)

The National Basketball Association is a professional basketball league composed of thirty teams in North America. Visit the official Web site: www.nba.com.

Teams in the Eastern Division

Atlanta Hawks
Boston Celtics
Charlotte Bobcats
Chicago Bulls
Cleveland Cavaliers
Detroit Pistons
Indiana Pacers
Miami Heat
Milwaukee Bucks
New Jersey Nets
New York Knicks
Orlando Magic
Philadelphia 76ers
Toronto Raptors
Washington Wizards

Teams in the Western Division

Dallas Mavericks
Denver Nuggets
Golden State Warriors
Houston Rockets
Los Angeles Clippers
Los Angeles Lakers
Memphis Grizzlies
Minnesota Timberwolves
New Orleans Hornets
Phoenix Suns
Portland Trail Blazers
Oklahoma City Thunder
Sacramento Kings
San Antonio Spurs
Utah Jazz

BASKETBALL ORGANIZATIONS

Aside from the NBA and WNBA, here are a number of organizations that may interest coaches, players, and parents.

AAU

www.aausports.org

Amateur Athletic Union is one of the largest, nonprofit, volunteer sports organizations in the United States. It is a multisport organization that is dedicated to the promotion and development of amateur sports and physical fitness programs. Programs offered are the AAU Junior Olympic Games and the President's Council on Physical Fitness and Sports.

Basketball Hall of Fame

www.hoophall.com

The Basketball Hall of Fame is an informational and educational resource center to showcase basketball today.

CYO

Catholic Youth Organization was founded to provide a service to t youth community. Its objective is to provide opportunities for you people to be involved in competition to develop physical fitne self-discipline, and positive attitudes of sportsmanship. Teams centered in parishes and/or Catholic and Christian schools. All spo are offered for children through eighth grade.

Hoop Group

www.hoopgroup.com

This site is the ultimate in East Coast youth basketball informatic including information about player camps, coaches, clinics, a tournaments.

NCAA

www.ncaa.org

National Collegiate Athletic Association is a collegiate basketball governing body that consists of coaches from all three divisions of the NCAA, which sets the rules for college basketball play. Basketball in the NCAA is divided into three divisions: Divisions 1, 2, and 3.

Nike Elite Youth Division

http://inside.nikebasketball.com

This division of Nike is dedicated to providing a platform for the finest basketball players in the nation and to making a positive impact on the best players in the country by providing elite tournaments, clinics, and all-star games.

USA Basketball

www.usabasketball.com

This organization is recognized for U.S. teams participating in international competitions.

Women's Basketball Hall of Fame

www.wbhof.com

The Women's Basketball Hall of Fame is an informational and educational resource center to showcase women's basketball today and to provide fun for all fans of women's basketball.

YBOA

www.yboa.org

Youth Basketball of America is an international governing body that promotes youth basketball worldwide. YBOA offers league development, tournaments, uniforms, educational clinics, scholarship programs, support materials, and insurance programs.

CHECKLISTS

It's important to come prepared for both practices and games. Here are checklists to make sure that you and your players remember what to bring.

Player Gear

- ❑ Ankle supports/knee pads
- ❑ Basketball
- ❑ Hair tie (girls)
- ❑ Headband/prewrap
- ❑ Sneakers
- ❑ Socks
- ❑ Sports bra
- ❑ Sports drink/water
- ❑ Sports slippers for after
- ❑ Sweatband
- ❑ Under Armour tank top to wear under uniform
- ❑ Uniform shorts
- ❑ Uniform top

Coach Practice Checklist

- ❑ Ball bag to carry balls
- ❑ Basketballs—at least six
- ❑ Cell phone
- ❑ Cones for drills
- ❑ Dry-erase board
- ❑ Emergency forms
- ❑ First-aid kit
- ❑ Practice schedule
- ❑ Reversible pinnies
- ❑ Stopwatch to time drills
- ❑ Towel
- ❑ Whistle

Game Checklist

- ❏ Basketballs and ball bag
- ❏ Emergency forms: Folders of contact information
- ❏ Extra uniform in case of blood
- ❏ First-aid kit
- ❏ Game ball that is new and inflated properly
- ❏ Proper coaches' attire
- ❏ Scorebook
- ❏ Scouting report
- ❏ Water bottles

Tryout Checklist

- ❏ Basketballs—at least twelve. Many kids will be trying out.
- ❏ Clipboard
- ❏ Cones
- ❏ Evaluation sheets
- ❏ Handout of an overview of season for parents
- ❏ Registration forms
- ❏ Tryout numbers and pins
- ❏ Whistle

GLOSSARY

Backdoor Cuts: A very basic play where a player quickly cuts toward the basket and receives a pass from teammate who has the ball.

Backpack: Following the player setting the screen for a double screen.

Ball side: Refers to the side of the floor where the ball is.

Block: The area directly under the rim, designated by two hash marks along the outside of the "key".

Blocking: An illegal move by a defender to impede the ball handler by making contact.

Bookkeeper: Person at the scorer's table that keeps record of fou points, timeouts, and running score.

Box and One: Box and one is when the best player on the opposi team is face guarded and the other four players play a zone defen in a box formation.

Butt Kicks: Use to stretch out quad muscles by kicking feet up butt area.

Charging: A personal foul committed when an offensive player il gally contacts a defensive player who has established position or stationary.

Close Out: Refers to the method in which a defender quickly slides up to and contains the ball handler or ball receiver.

Dead Ball: Occurs whenever the whistle blows to stop play and after a field goal, but before the opponent gains possession of the ball.

Defensive Slides: Player should stay low, not have legs crossed, feet should be a shoulder width apart, arms are slightly away from body at waist level, palms facing up, back is straight, knees bent, and hands should not touch floor while sliding.

Denying: Preventing your man from getting the ball.

Elbow: Intersection of the free throw line and the side of the key.

Flagrant Foul: When a player purposely fouls a player with intent to injure the player or the foul could injure the player. This type of foul happens when a player doesn't make a legitimate play for ball and holds, pushes, or grabs the offensive player.

Free Throws: The person that is fouled takes their place behind the free throw line (15 feet from the basket). All other players must stand in their correct places until the ball leaves the shooter's hands.

High Knees: Also called running-in-place, a player should bring hi[s] knees up to his chest area.

Jab Step: A common foot fake which, depending on the defensive player's reaction, is used to set up either a drive or jump shot.

Key Area: The area bordered by two angled lines between the fre[e] throw and end lines, indicated by a separate color on the floor. N[o] offensive player may stand in the key area for more than three sec[-]onds at a time. Also known as the lane or the paint.

On the Ball Defense: Defending the player with the ball.

Grapevine Exercise: Stand with your feet together. Using your right foot take one step to the right then step behind your right foot with your left foot. Cross your left leg behind your right leg and place your left foot behind and slightly to the right of your right foot. Your left foot should be pointing toward your right heel but not directly behind it. Take a step to the right with your right foot bringing your feet together again. Continue exercise.

Help Defense: Sagging off your man to help your teammates prevent inside "penetration".

One and One Foul Shots: These foul shots are taken when a team is in the bonus. If players make the first shot they are awarded a second shot. If player misses then the ball is considered live.

Over the Back: Occurs when a player reaches over another player for a rebound and there is contact. The defensive player must have established position.

Post-Up: To establish position in the low post, the area near the basket below the foul line, usually in order to take advantage of a small defender.

Press Breaker: A play designed to counteract the full court press.

Reaching In: When a player goes for a steal, but touches the body of the offensive player.

Screen: A blocking move by an offensive player, by standing beside or behind a defender, to free a teammate to shoot, receive pass, or drive to score. The offensive player setting the screen must remain stationary.

Top of Key: Area above the free throw circle.

Transition: The process of changing from defense to offense or vice versa.

Triple Threat Position: When a player receives the ball, they go into this ready position. This position gives you three options of being ready to shoot, pass, or drive. It helps players also see the floor, give a look into post, and help see the defense.

Up Screen: The low post teammate will move up, vertically, and set a screen on the high post teammate's defender.

Weak Side: The opposite side away from the ball.

INDEX